CAN THE CHURCH FIND ITS VOICE AGAIN

CRY
REPENT

M. K. GANTT

FROM THE AUTHOR OF CRY MERCY

Cry Repent

Can the Church Find Her Voice Again?

M. K. Gantt

The Author of Cry Mercy!

Foreword by
Dr. David Berman, B.A, Th.M, Th.D

mkgantt.com
Publications
Brattleboro, Vermont

IV

Copyright © 2019 Michael K Gantt

Michael K. Gantt

539 Western Avenue

Brattleboro, VT 05301

Printed in the United States

ISBN: 9781093264494

Available from Amazon.com

And

www.mkgantt.com/books

Dedication

This book is dedicated to the thousands of faithful pastors and evangelists, missionaries, Bible teachers, and Christian workers across America and around the world who preach the gospel without compromise and without apology. Few know, and even fewer understand, the incredible personal sacrifice they make for the sake of the Gospel; *the power of God unto salvation.*

I also want to acknowledge the hundreds of thousands of believers around the globe who are enduring terrible hardship and persecution because they refuse to deny the Name of Christ. Christians are the most persecuted people group on the planet and the price of faithfulness for many is rape, torture, and death.

Let their suffering and death not be in vain. Let us forever be faithful to the cause of Christ until His appearing, whereupon He will establish His eternal Kingdom, forever and ever, Amen.

MARANATHA

x

Available from Amazon.com and

www.mkgantt.com/books

Endorsements

Michael Gantt's book *Cry Repent* does not soft-pedal what America needs and why. Like the Hebrew prophets of old did with Israel and the nations around her, Michael points to our sins—our moral and spiritual failings, our intolerable rebellion against the holy and righteous God. Michael also tells us the remedy: contrite and honest confession, throwing ourselves onto the mercy of God; turning away from our sin; and embracing divine forgiveness through the righteous sacrifice of Jesus Christ. Apart from this, all we can expect is divine judgment and wrath—justice bearing down on us from on high. Read. Repent. Give away this book as you tell others the truth about our nation, themselves, their need, and the solution. Maybe God will spare our nation.

William D. Watkins, theologian, philosopher, speaker, editor, and award-winning writer; president of Literary Solutions

Books like this are often hard to like. But I love this one. Michael Gantt is a superb storyteller and weaves a tough message we all need to hear into well–told stories throughout this book. His call to the church in America is profound, clear, and articulate. And his voice is both uniquely inviting and powerfully compelling.

Peter Lundell, pastor, writer, teacher, life coach

Like a prophet of old, Michael Gantt's voice cries out in the wilderness of American political, economic, ecclesiastical and family moral culture, with a simple message *"Repent!"* Not only does he diagnose the foundation of the ills of our cultural demise, he also offers the only inoculation or antidote needed to bring about true lasting change. With compelling and illustrative story-telling, Michael drives home clearly the message the Lord has burdened him to deliver. While he focuses on the nation of America, the Biblical principles he shares are equally relevant for any nation or people. This book, *Cry Repent*, will challenge all who read, and hopefully inspire other princes, prophets, priests and people to heed the message and with faith and boldness find and articulate the voice of God again as they stand in the gap for this generation.

Dr. Ronald L. Bernier, Senior Pastor
Master Builder Ministries

A prophet translates God's words into the language of contemporary culture. In *Cry Repent*, my friend and brother in ministry of twenty-two years, Michael Gantt, is calling American Christians to hear, apply, and loudly repeat Jesus' message of repentance and transformation life. The urgent need of a compromised Church and a broken culture compels the author as Christ calls us to genuine, meaningful repentance through his message.

Pastor Charles Tyree,
Norwich Alliance Church

Cry Repent clearly calls out for men and women with contrite and repentance spirit to rise up to intercede for America. Powerful, riveting, and gut wrenching...

William Levi, Founder and Overseer
Operation Nehemiah Missions & the Nile Beth Israel
Messianic Congregation

"When the prodigal son was hungry he went to feed upon husks, but when he was starving, he turned to his father." Martyn Lloyd-Jones.

Mike Gantt, a personal friend, and fellow pastor, colorfully explains the doctrine of repentance. A "Change of mind" that leads to a "Change of Action." He reminds us that true hope lies in the heart of man releasing his will to the lordship of Christ. It has always been God's message but it has been diminished and diluted in our churches.

Mike makes it clear, it is time to "Fish or Cut Bait." I giggled a few times at Mike's country down to earth style of writing. He challenges us to live the life that God has always desired for His children. Well written and timely.

Dr. Duffy Johnson
Pastor, Christian School Administrator

Without repentance, we have no lamp stand, no hope, no light for our future. Like John the Baptist of old, God will inspire His messenger to cry, "Repent," because the kingdom of Heaven is at hand, a promise is coming, and we must be baptized into repentance in order to receive the promise. Michael Gantt is modern-day messenger and a worthy watchman who lights a candle in our present darkness in America and cries, "Repent!" If you believe God will bring revival, if you are leaning forward into the wind to watch the next great awakening in America, this book is for you.

C. Hope Flinchbaugh
Author and Intercessor

Table of Contents

Foreword

When I was young I remember vividly there being a consciousness of moral right and wrong in the culture. Believe me when I tell you I was under no delusion back then about Man's destructive behavior toward others or himself since it was obvious. For sin, manifested in one way or another, has always been with us since Adam fell from his communion with Almighty God into the abyss of self with all its pride, arrogance and its trappings. My memories are not some long lost desire to relive my childhood since I had a very bad childhood. My family was fine. A strong father and traditional Mother who both loved me and my three brothers and sister. We were poor but that was not a problem. It was instead the fact that for many years I was terribly persecuted because I am a Jew.

My purpose in telling you this is to make sure you understand I am not making my comments based on a perfect childhood as though I dwelled in "Mayberry R.F.D". Sure many romance their childhood and that often comes from a strong desire for times when things seemed simpler. I assure you that is not my motivation as I write this forward. Every generation laments the passing of old ways. We remember how we used to do this or that, the cars we drove, the places we went that no longer exist, and of course certain feelings which are indescribable to anyone but those who lived it with us. My focus really has nothing to do with that at all.

What we see today is not the normal older generation lamenting the various pop culture changes like different music, clothes or ways of doing things. It's not a simple "In my day we would" (fill in the blank). Instead what we have in this confused day is a total rejection of the basis of our thinking. We have gone from thesis/antithesis thinking (the Judeo Christian world view based on the Word of God), to a relativistic worldview (mankind's feelings and fleshly desires now being almighty god) with personal restraint that only comes from an individual's relativistic feelings. Mind you, I am not saying we used to follow the Word of God in every way, far from it. It was more a general sense from which our overall world view was gathered. In other words, we may have sinned as all humans do, but we knew it was wrong. We had a basis, a starting point, a sort of aroma in the air that reminded us that what we were doing was wrong or right. I was not a Christian. I am a Jew who at that time did not know the Lord Jesus Christ. Yet even in my unregenerate state, I at least understood from Creation's evidence that there is an almighty God. That knowledge did not at that time inform me enough to repent and come to Jesus. However, it certainly informed my conscience concerning certain behaviors and matters of honor.

Relativism is the enemy of repentance. It is the great open door to self-deception concerning literally everything. What a hoax, a terrible impractical joke, a road map for destruction it is. You see, when one has a relativistic deception controlling their mind, the concept of true repentance disappears. Yes they can self-realize they did something wrong or right, but the wrong or rights does not come from an ultimate authority from outside of them. It instead comes from their own fluid sense of what is good and what is not. This is a radical change in thinking that has brought death and destruction far, deep, and wide in our culture. Relativism begs two questions; "If wrong and right are both determined by the individual's own human intellect with all of its confusion, what is there to repent of? And what does that make us? Clearly its implication convinces us that we are our own god. If we are our own god, there is no need for true repentance.

Michael K. Gantt understands this problem well. I have known Rev. Gantt for 20 years. I like to refer to Michael's family as the gospel family. Both he, and his family have impacted many with the love of Jesus for decades. His son Bryan is also a fine preacher and pastor. For decades Pastor Gantt has given his strength to the propagation of the gospel of Jesus Christ. He has been a voice along with few others crying in the spiritual wilderness of post-modern culture. This post-modernism has not only impacted culture, it has also decimated the influence and spiritual power of the church.

Michael is my Christian brother, friend, and co-laborer in the kingdom of God and he is a rare find indeed. I wish the "rare find" part was not so. I am sure he wishes the same. Our cry as committed Gospel preachers is not a plea to return to the music we loved, the clothes we wore, or the places we loved that are gone.

Ours is the same call every preacher has made since John the Baptist; "Prepare ye the way of the Lord."

Michael K. Gantt cries repentance to the world, and has done so for decades. However, the real gut-wrenching cry he makes is to the church. A prophet in the sense of the New Testament, Michael has the prophetic guts to speak things most are afraid to speak knowing his words often find ears that do not want to hear. He does this that he may by God's grace alone shake us from our slumber.

Michael K. Gantt is not simply a talker, a man sitting on a high horse pontificating philosophical mumbo-jumbo and passing it off as theology. He cuts right through the high mindedness, pride, and arrogance that has led most of the church in America to compromise with post-modern relativism. He lays out before us the clear problem and the only solution. In every generation, because God loves His church, he raises up men with guts to take the heat and bring conscience back to His people by the Holy Ghost. Pastor Gantt is one of those men. I implore us all to listen. Don't merely hear, cheer and lament, but rather to hear cheer, and repent. Let us heed the words of this man of God. We shall all be better for it.

Rev. David M. Berman B.A, Th.M., Th.D.

PREFACE

I want to make a simple appeal to anyone who reads this book. I have made use of large portions of Scripture in this little book. I have been counseled that I should paraphrase or "tell the story" of some of the passages because I am told, "Your readers will skim over long passages of Scripture."

In *Cry Repent*, I have rejected that counsel, not because I don't respect those who lend their wisdom to me, for I most certainly do highly regard their wisdom and counsel. I have rejected their counsel because I do not believe there can be greater text put to paper than the holy Word of God.

If anything, the reader should give a greater weight to the words of the Scriptures, showing infinitely greater preference for the word of holy men of God who were moved by the Holy Spirit to write down the thoughts of God.

So, should you come upon a passage of Scripture that is longer than you are accustomed to reading; resist the temptation to skip over that part. Read every word of it–twice if necessary, to get it all. It is a trap of the enemy that would lead you to believe that my words could somehow carry greater importance or demand more attention than the words of the apostles and prophets.

We live in a generation in which the Word of God is considered far more lightly than did generations that went before us. This is to our great, great loss.

I urge you not to think that there might be more meat in my words than in the words of the Bible. Every principle, every concept that I put forth in this book, I believe I have received under the unction of the Holy Spirit, and I have endeavored to fasten down each idea with the weight of Scripture.

"All scripture is given by inspiration of God, and is profitable for doctrine, for reproof, for correction, for instruction in righteousness: That the man of God may be perfect, thoroughly furnished unto all good works" (2 Timothy 3:16–17 KJV)

1 | A Reluctant Messenger

Rough, calloused hands grasped his arms. The hardened sailors were silent, but resolute, as they pushed him toward the railing of the ship. The mighty vessel tossed about like a leaf in the wind. Huge breakers crashed over the bow. The mainmast had already broken, snapping like a twig, and with each new swell the ship's timbers groaned under the pressure. One sailor stumbled as a huge wave crashed upon the deck. He screamed in terror as the massive wall of water swept him to his death. His scream was instantly lost in the howl of the fierce wind.

As the men grasped Jonah's arms and feet they struggled to maintain enough balance to pick him up. Faces leathered by years at sea were filled with dread at what they were about to do and yet, they had no choice. This man was being pursued by his God, a God who seemed entirely willing to destroy them all in that pursuit. The ship's mate looked at him and mouthed the words, "I'm sorry." He nodded to the crew who lifted him above the ship's rail and heaved him into the sea.

Jonah did not fall into the sea. The rolling swells reached up and took him, drawing him into their embrace. Even as the cascading waves enveloped him, he could sense the storm had already begun to weaken. The ship would be safe and he would not be responsible for the deaths of those souls.

Jonah had tried to run from God. As his body was tossed and contorted by the swirling waters, Jonah realized that his flight from Joppa toward Tarshish was foolish. Had not the beloved King David declared,

"Where shall I go from your Spirit? Or where shall I flee from your presence? If I ascend to heaven, you are there! If I make my bed in Sheol, you are there! If I take the wings of the morning and dwell in the uttermost parts of the sea, even there your hand shall lead me, and your right hand shall hold me. If I say, 'Surely the darkness shall cover me, and the light about me be night,' even the darkness is not dark to you; the night is bright as the day for darkness is as light with you" (Psalm 139:7-12 ESV).

God had instructed Jonah to travel to the wicked Assyrians of Nineveh to announce His judgment upon them. The Assyrians were a vile and bloodthirsty people and Jonah hated them. Why would God warn them? Even a warning of impending judgment was an act of mercy for which Jonah considered the Assyrians to be unworthy. Why didn't God just rain fire upon them as He did at Sodom and Gomorrah?

Or maybe ... maybe the earth could just open to swallow them up, sucking them and their wickedness directly to hell. Even as his lungs burned from a lack of oxygen his mind was consumed with his hatred for the Assyrians.

As consciousness began to slip away, in that brief space as one transitions from life to death, Jonah thought he could see the face of Elijah. He remembered when as a young boy in Zarephath, the old prophet would visit his home. Once, he was awakened from a deep sleep to discover the old man lying on top of him crying out to God that he might live. He remembered so clearly the raspy voice of the old prophet, *"O Lord my God, let this child's life come into him again"* (1 Kings 17:21 ESV). He had not been asleep at all. He had died from a fever and the old man had commanded life back into his body.

Jonah was no longer a boy in Zarephath. He was a rebellious prophet of Israel, fleeing the presence of God. Even in the stormy waters of this raging sea, Jonah sensed something sweep by him. He opened his eyes to see what it might be. There, through the murk, he could see a fast-moving shape making a long sweeping turn in his direction. At first, he was sure he could see the face of the old prophet again, moving toward him, growing larger and larger. Elijah's mouth opened, and Jonah thought he might speak. Instead, his mouth became wider and wider. Jonah's blood froze, realizing that

3

it was not Elijah at all. It was a giant sea creature swimming directly toward him, spreading his massive jaws wide. Jonah's last thought before losing consciousness was, *"Where shall I flee from your presence?"*

Jonah slowly opened his eyes. Consciousness was creeping back into his brain. He didn't know where he was; he was enveloped in utter darkness. But, he could breathe. He was alive. He was no longer being swept about by strong ocean currents. Then, he remembered that fish. It would seem that God was so angry with him that simply drowning in the sea was not a vile enough death for a rebellious prophet. God had a slower, more terrifying, and more painful death in mind for him. He was in the belly of a giant fish slowing being digested while still alive.

As he lay within the confines of the beast's stomach, a stark realization began to awaken in his addled brain. "I'm not dead. I was cast into the sea and I did not drown. I was swallowed by a fish and I have not died. I am alive!" Occasionally, the fish would open his massive mouth and Jonah would be bathed in the intake of seaweed, plankton, and fish. With each moment that he remained alive, hope began to rise within him. From deep within the bowels of the mighty leviathan Jonah began to pray.

"In trouble, deep trouble, I prayed to GOD.

He answered me.

From the belly of the grave I cried, 'Help!'

You heard my cry.

You threw me into ocean's depths,

into a watery grave,

With ocean waves, ocean breakers

crashing over me.

I said, 'I've been thrown away,

thrown out, out of your sight.

I'll never again lay eyes

on your Holy Temple.'

Ocean gripped me by the throat.

The ancient Abyss grabbed me and held tight.

My head was all tangled in seaweed

at the bottom of the sea where the mountains take root.

I was as far down as a body can go,

and the gates were slamming shut behind
me forever—

Yet you pulled me up from that grave alive,

O GOD, my God!

When my life was slipping away,

I remembered GOD,

And my prayer got through to you. . .

(Jonah 2:2-7 MSG)

Two men walked together along the water's edge just south of Tarsus, on the outer rim of the massive Assyrian empire. As they walked, one of them spotted a large sea creature that had beached itself on the shore. Thinking that if the creature was not long dead it would provide much food for their families, they prepared themselves to harvest as much meat as possible. As they drew closer to the massive creature, it began to convulse with powerful heaves. They stood with curious amazement as waves of water, partially digested fish, and seaweed were vomited onto the beach. They realized they probably would not be able to harvest the flesh from this great fish to eat as he was clearly very sick with some sort of disease.

The stench of his regurgitation was growing more and more pungent as they drew closer. They stopped short as they heard a soft groan—a groan that did not come from the creature but from the heap of waste the fish had vomited. Slowly, out of the tangle of fish carcasses and seaweed, something stirred and then, with great effort rose to stand on two feet.

It was a man!

He stood there, covered in putrefied seaweed and fish guts, staggering, barely able to maintain his balance. His clothing, or what was left of it, was in tatters having been soaked for days in the digestive juices of the great sea creature. The hair on his head was gone, save for a few wispy strands. He had no body hair at all; no eyebrows, no eyelashes, or beard. His skin was pasty white and sagged loosely as the outer layers were beginning to peel away.

Slowly, the man pulled gobs of sopping seaweed from his head and face and strained as his eyes grew accustomed to the bright sunlight after having been three days in total darkness. He saw the two men standing a few yards away, slack-jawed and in terror at the sight they had just seen. After a few moments he spoke, or at least he tried to speak. It was more guttural than actual language.

"N...n...i...nuh...v...v...uh."

He cleared his throat violently and vomited up a mixture of salt water and blood. The man slumped over, hands on his knees trying to breathe, trying to speak. He finally pushed out the words, "Nineveh...which way?"

One of the men, unable to speak, pointed a trembling finger eastward. The man nodded his head, raised himself up, and with a huge sigh turned eastward, toward Nineveh.

When Jonah was sent to the work of the Lord,

The outlook was not very bright;

He never had done such a hard thing before,

So he backed and ran off from the fight.

But God sent a big fish to swallow him up,

The story I'm sure you all know;

He did not compel him to go 'gainst his will,

But He just made him willing to go.

(From "The Hornet Song," Author Unknown)

Jonah trudged across the hot desert sands to Nineveh. Huge city that it was, it was a three day walk from one side to the other. God had given him a simple message to deliver. "Yet forty days, and Nineveh shall be overthrown!" (Jonah 3:4 ESV).

Only eight words. No introduction, no sermon, no amusing anecdotes, no altar call, no apology, no subtlety, no permission asked and none granted. It was a cold, direct pronouncement of impending judgment; the response of a holy God to their wickedness. Jonah traversed the broad expanse of the city, one side to the other, whereupon he left the city and retired to a hillside overlooking Nineveh where he could bear witness to the wrath of God. His hatred for the inhabitants of Nineveh swelled up in his heart almost to the point of glee as he sat in anticipation of the apocalyptic wrath that would soon befall them. He waited and waited...and waited...but the fire did not fall. Judgment did not come because something remarkable had happened in Nineveh.

The people of Nineveh believed God. They called for a fast and put on sackcloth, from the greatest of them to the least of them. The word reached the king of Nineveh, and he arose from his throne, removed his robe, covered himself with sackcloth, and sat in ashes. And he issued a proclamation and published through Nineveh, *"By*

9

the decree of the king and his nobles: Let neither man nor beast, herd nor flock, taste anything. Let them not feed or drink water, but let man and beast be covered with sackcloth, and let them call out mightily to God. Let everyone turn from his evil way and from the violence that is in his hands. Who knows? God may turn and relent and turn from his fierce anger, so that we may not perish" (Jonah 3:5-9 ESV).

Nineveh was a cruel and bloodthirsty city known and feared throughout the region. The Assyrians had troubled Israel for centuries, entrenching itself as not only an enemy of the nation of Israel, but the God of Israel as well. It is understandable that Jonah would have reveled in witnessing the overthrow of Nineveh. Yet, in response to a plain, direct warning from the prophet's lips, the inhabitants of the city humbled themselves before Yahweh, and cried out to Him for mercy. Nineveh was spared.

Jonah had walked through a gate on one side of the city, and what a sight he must have been to the Ninevites. He was a hairless, bleached out, partially digested ghoul who walked a straight line through the city repeating over and over again the same eight words, *"Yet forty days, and Nineveh shall be overthrown!"* The prophet did not edit or editorialize God's message to Nineveh. It was God's message, not his. Jonah did not expound or exegete.

He did not engage in debate. He did not cajole or plead. He did not present himself as a "friend" of the people of Nineveh. He made no effort to fit in or become relevant to their culture. He expressed no compassion, no love, and no pity for the people. His was by no means a *seeker sensitive* ministry.

Jonah was on a mission from God. He had a word from God to deliver. He had a warning to give; a raw, uncooked meal with no niceties or accoutrements. There was no effort to make the people feel better about themselves, to affirm them, or to minimize their condition or jeopardy. He did not couch his message in any form of subtlety, nor did he sing all the verses of "Just As I Am," twice.

This was as stark, unappealing, ingratiating, and classless as a message can be. Jonah looked Nineveh in the eye and spat out the hard, unvarnished truth; a warning that contained just those eight blunt words, "Yet forty days, and Nineveh shall be overthrown!"

The United States of America is living in the shadow of the judgment of God and we need a Jonah.

2 | It's the Message

There has never been a less appealing messenger from God than Jonah. Many preachers have arrived to preach at a meeting; travel weary, unkempt, disheveled—overworked and under rested. But none of us have ever traveled to a meeting in the digestive system of a fish, partially digested and totally repulsive in appearance and odor.

If Jonah's odor was bad, his attitude was worse. To his core, he hated the Assyrians. It was his loathing for the people of Nineveh that landed him in that fish in the first place. He could think of no news that would be more welcomed in Israel than the annihilation of the Ninevites. He could imagine nothing more loathsome than some prophet rushing to Nineveh to warn them of impending destruction. Most detestable to Jonah was the moment when God directed HIM to go to Nineveh to warn the city that He was about to destroy them.

Jonah arrived at the gate of the huge city, ready to obey God. It was a joyless, begrudging obedience. He obeyed not because he had a newfound affection for the people of Nineveh but because three days in the belly of a fish had convinced him that Yahweh, for whatever reason, was determined to warn the people of Nineveh.

Jonah brings to mind the story told many times of the little boy who was being disobedient to his mother. The exasperated mom finally spoke to him in her most stern voice, "You go sit down on that stool in the corner and don't you move until I tell you to!" Shoulders drooped, eyebrows scrunched together, lower lip pouted out as the boy shuffled toward the corner. Arms crossed and eyes aflame with rebellion, he slammed his derriere down upon the stool. As his mother walked away, he shot back, "I am sitting down on the outside, but on the inside, I'm still standing up!"

As Jonah strode through the western most gate of the city he was surely sitting down on the inside. He was not there for the benefit of the people of Nineveh but as an act of his own self-preservation. He would deliver God's message like a mailman called in to work on Christmas day. God had given him an eight-word message, and an eight-word message he would deliver. There would be no amusing illustrations to make the message more palatable, no warm familial stories to engage his audience emotionally. He made no effort to exegete or expand on the various points of God's message. In fact, there were no points to expound upon.

Just...eight...words.

"Yet forty days, and Nineveh shall be overthrown!" From the gate of entry he walked a day's journey where he began to deliver his message; all the way to the gate of exit he shouts it over and over again. There is no record of Jonah engaging in conversation or debate with any of the residents. There is no record of any instructions given as to how they might avoid the terrible fate he had announced. It was cold, passionless, and compassionless; no effort to convince, or win, to woo, draw or convert. Message delivered, Jonah swept out of the easternmost gate, slamming the door as he left, his demeanor oozing contempt. I can imagine him muttering under his breath, *"There. I've delivered the message as ordered. Now, to hell with every one of you!"*

Striding to a nearby hillside where he would be able to observe, but far enough away to be safe when the destruction came, he sat down to wait for the hand of God to strike.

Of course, destruction never came. The record in the Bible is clear. The people of Nineveh from the greatest to the least believed Jonah's warning. They were convinced in their hearts that the wrath of God was indeed approaching and they responded with a great wave of repentance, pleading with God for mercy. Jonah's worst fear came to pass—God did hear their prayers and He did respond by sparing the city.

What caused such a remarkable change of heart? It certainly wasn't Jonah, for he offered no hope. His disdain for them could not have been more obvious. The fact that he was there at all was due to God's extraordinary pressure brought to bear upon His prophet. He clearly was not there out of compassion for the city.

We do not celebrate Jonah, nor do we ascribe any great valor or spirituality to this rebellious prophet. He was disobedient, angry, petulant, and willing to die rather than deliver the message of God to Nineveh. However, we can learn from Jonah that the power is in the Word of God, the message, rather than in the man. God anoints a man for a specific ministry, but His power is found in His Word. *"So shall my word be that goeth forth out of my mouth: it shall not return unto me void, but it shall accomplish that which I please, and it shall prosper in the thing wherto I sent it"* (Isaiah 55:11 KJV).

"For the word of God is quick and powerful, and sharper than any two-edged sword, piercing

even to the dividing asunder of soul and spirit, and of the joints and marrow, and is a discerner of the thoughts and intents of the heart" (Hebrews 4:12 KJV).

"For I am not ashamed of the gospel of Christ: for it is the power of god unto salvation" (Romans 1:16 KJV).

"He sent his word, and healed them, and delivered them from their destructions" (Psalm 107:20 KJV).

To be clear: Jonah did not deliver Nineveh—God did. It was God's word. It was God's message. It was God's power that brought conviction which brought the city of Nineveh to a place of humility before Him.

Many times throughout the Bible we see God choose and use men of questionable ability or integrity. He often chooses the smallest, weakest, or meanest to carry his message. He chooses men with no message of their own, no personal agenda to achieve, no personal power or charisma to put on display. When Peter and John were dragged before the Sanhedrin in Acts 4 they were marked as "unlearned and ignorant men."

When Peter stood on the Day of Pentecost to preach his message was simple. At the heart of it: Jesus, God's Anointed One, has been crucified—and you did it. The response of the crowd was immediate and urgent: *"Men and brethren, what shall we do?"* Peter's answer was as blunt as his message, *"Repent, and be baptized every one of you in the name of Jesus Christ for the remission of sins, and ye shall receive the gift of the Holy Ghost"* (Acts 2:38 KJV).

Solomon prophesied on the occasion of the dedication of the Temple, *"If my people who are called by my name humble themselves, and pray and seek my face and turn from their wicked ways, then I will hear from heaven and will forgive their sin and heal their land"* (2 Chronicles 7:14 ESV).

The Prophet Ezekiel cried, *"For I take no pleasure in the death of anyone, declares the Sovereign Lord. Repent and live!"* (Ezekiel 18:32 NIV).

"Come near to God and he will come near to you. Wash your hands, you sinners, and purify your hearts, you double-minded" (James 4:8 NIV)

Zechariah trumpets the cry of the heart of God, *"Return to me,' declares the Lord Almighty, and I will return to you,' says the Lord Almighty"* (Zechariah 1:3 NIV).

John the Apostle pleads, *"If we confess our sins, he is faithful to forgive us our sins and to cleanse us from all unrighteousness"* (1 John 1:9 ESV).

The United States of America is living in the shadow of the judgment of God, and He has given us the message that, if heeded, will turn away his wrath from the nation: *Turn, purify, confess, repent.*

Jonah was given a simple message to deliver to Nineveh: "Yet forty days, and Nineveh shall be overthrown." Jonah delivered that message, unvarnished and undecorated, and the people of Nineveh heard it, they believed it, and they cried out to God for mercy.

It would appear that the church no longer believes in the sufficiency of the Holy Scriptures to reach and change men's hearts. It is not the Word of God plus fog machines and pulsating lights. It is not the Word of God plus rock music and humanistic psychology. It is not the Word of God plus anything.

All Scripture is breathed out by God and profitable for teaching, for reproof, for correction, and for training in righteousness" (2 Timothy 3:16 ESV).

For the word of God is living and active, sharper than any two-edged sword, piercing to the division of soul and of spirit, of joints and of marrow, and discerning the thoughts and intentions of the heart (Hebrews 4:12 ESV).

If the church of the Lord Jesus Christ in America today is to be true to its calling, we will begin to sound the warning from coast to coast, from border to border. The wrath of God is upon us and unless we acknowledge our sin and turn from our wickedness, America will be overthrown.

The message must be delivered without nuance, without subtlety, without regard for the howling response of sinners, without fearing the loss of our tax-exempt status, and unconcerned that we might be prosecuted and imprisoned. It must be delivered with an absolute confidence that the power of God is in His Word and not in the method or the man. Time is short and the stakes are high.

My friend Paul Jehle says, *"The problem with the church today in America is that it has a hunger and desire to be famous, to have their leaders' names in lights, and to be revered by the world because of how smart and powerful we are"* (Dr. Paul Jehle, The New Testament Church of Cedarville, Plymouth Rock Foundation).

Before America can come to a place of humility before God, the church must be restored to its own place of humility. If our desire is to be revered by the world, we will never bring the warning to repent. We have left our watchman's post on the wall and joined the party.

The persecution of the church in China grows. Pastor Wang Yi, leader of the Early Rain Church, has been arrested along with more than 100 of his members. In the face of his impending arrest,

Yi wrote an impassioned letter to the church. Part of the text reads:

As a pastor, my firm belief in the gospel, my teaching, and my rebuking of all evil proceeds from Christ's command in the gospel and from the unfathomable love of that glorious King. Every man's life is extremely short, and God fervently commands the church to lead and call any man to repentance who is willing to repent. Christ is eager and willing to forgive all who turn from their sins. This is the goal of all the efforts of the church in China—to testify to the world about our Christ, to testify to the Middle Kingdom about the Kingdom of Heaven, to testify to earthly, momentary lives about heavenly, eternal life. This is also the pastoral calling that I have received. ("Letter from a Chengdu Jail by Wang Yi," CBNNews.com December 16, 2018 by Steve Warren.)

We are long past the seeker sensitive era and we have outlived the consumeristic shopping mall church, and we can no longer afford the luxury of compromising the authority of the Scriptures in an effort to make ourselves more comfortable and accommodating to the sinful urges of men. We must once again be the church crying out to men, *"save yourselves from this crooked generation"* (Acts 2:40 ESV).

The church was birthed in adversity. It flourished despite the sword and the flames of

21

persecution. The message of the church was impactful in the culture because it was not a part of the culture; it was countercultural. The church was always meant to lay itself across the path of the culture, to interrupt the flow of culture, to stand in the way of the culture. The role of the church in culture is to bring the voice of God into the conversation of man; to, by all means, turn the tide of mankind away from its own self-destruction and toward God.

On January 1, 404 A.D, a monk by the name of Telemachus, traveled to Rome in order to encourage the churches in Rome. When he arrived, he heard about the gladiator fights in the coliseum. Having never witnessed such things, Telemachus went to the coliseum. He was shocked by the barbarism, and more so by the reaction of the crowds cheering on the gladiators, screaming with glee as each vanquished fighter was killed. Heartbroken, Telemachus leaped onto the floor of the coliseum and ran to stand between two of the fighters, pleading with them that they would stop the bloodshed. The crowd and the gladiators were so enraged by his meddling in their "games," Telemachus was slain on the spot. His body was then pelted with stones hurled by the audience.

History records though, that Telemachus' death was not in vain. Witnessing the murder of this holy man sent shockwaves through the coliseum.

Stunned silence gripped the stadium as men left one by one, in silence. God had used the zeal and courage of one man to change the course of history. The Romans abandoned their gladiator games from that day forward (*Foxe's Book of Martyrs*).

Telemachus did not flow with the culture but threw himself across the path of the culture and, in this instance, turned the tide of the culture. Like Telemachus and like Pastor Wang Yi we must be once again willing to stand in the path of the culture, or as Ezekiel said, to stand in the gap for the nation. We must run to the wall and interrupt the world's hilarious merrymaking to sound the alarm. Judgment is coming! The storm clouds of God's wrath are billowing on the horizon. Wake up! Wake up!

The spirit of Noah must once again rise within the church to warn of impending destruction, and we must not again be bullied into silence. Confession and repentance is the doorway to the Ark and there is no other way. There is no election that can save our nation. There is no president who can be our Savior. There is no judgment by the Supreme Court that can turn the tide of God's wrath.

Men may laugh and mock, they may arrest and imprison, they may kill us, they may throw the watchman from the wall—but so what? The warning must be sounded or the blood of millions will be on our hands. We must trust in the power of the Word of God and in the ability of the Holy Spirit to penetrate the sin-hardened hearts of the people of America.

"The word of the Lord came to me: Son of man, speak to your people and say to them, If I bring the sword upon a land, and the people of the land take a man from among them, and make him their watchman, and if he sees the sword coming upon the land and blows the trumpet and warns the people, then if anyone who hears the sound of the trumpet does not take warning, and the sword comes and takes him away, his blood shall be upon his own head. He heard the sound of the trumpet and did not take warning; his blood shall be upon himself. But if he had taken warning, he would have saved his life. But if the watchman sees the sword coming and does not blow the trumpet, so that the people are not warned, and the sword comes and takes any one of them, that person is taken away in his iniquity, but his blood I will require at the watchman's hand.

"So you, son of man, I have made a watchman for the house of Israel. Whenever you hear a word from my mouth, you shall give them warning from me. If I say to the wicked, O wicked one, you shall surely die, and you do not speak to warn the wicked to turn from his way, that wicked person shall die in his iniquity, but his blood I will

require at your hand. But if you warn the wicked to turn from his way, and he does not turn from his way, that person shall die in his iniquity, but you will have delivered your soul" (Ezekiel 33:1-9 ESV).

The watchman is not at his post to bring an appealing or an affirming message. The watchman is on the wall only to warn of impending danger. The culture hates it, but the church is not called to affirm perversion or immorality. The church is called to warn men of the danger that they face because of their sin. We are not called to go with the flow, to get in step with the culture. We are called to throw ourselves onto the floor of the arena and cry, "STOP!"

In an effort to be the church with a more appealing message we have become a church with no message. In soothing tones we have assured sinners that God loves them just like they are, but we have failed to instruct them that God has no intention of leaving them just like they are. We have not told them that He will dispatch the Holy Spirit and the Word of God to cleanse and transform, to change and deliver, to purify and sanctify to fulfill His will in us that we would be conformed to the image of His Son.

In China, they have *banned* the Bible. In America, we have *sanitized* the Bible. We have removed any and all words that might be found offensive to sinners. Under the weak hand of modern theologians the Bible in America has become the first transgender, polyamorous, sexually liberated holy book in history. The Bible has been edited and rewritten as a non-confrontational catalogue of moral fluidity. Instead of urging men to look into the mirror that is the Word of God that they might be changed into the image of Christ, we have rather peered into the wretched, tortured souls of men to reshape the revelation of God's Holy Self into a chronicle of the self-destruction of humanity.

The United States of America is living in the shadow of the judgment of God. We must once again trust in the power of the Word of God.

3 | Confession

This is the message God has given me for this hour. Though my flesh might hesitate, I cannot run away from it. The wrath of God is upon America. Unless we acknowledge our sin and turn from our wickedness, America will be overthrown.

In so many cases, the doctrine of confession and repentance is lost to the modern church. The world is enraged by the message of the gospel, and much of the church is terrified by the gospel, or embarrassed by the gospel, or has forgotten altogether what the gospel message really is. The idea of confession and repentance has been erased from our spiritual vocabulary and replaced with doctrines of self-love, self-esteem, and live your best life now. Yet, the Bible is clear that the core of human blessing is rooted in forgiveness of sins and our forgiveness is directly tied to the confession of our sins.

Confession is not telling God something He doesn't know. God is omniscient—He knows everything. He sees every wicked deed, every act of injustice, He hears every idle word and knows every vile thought. No, when we confess our sins we are not letting God in on some dirty secret. Confession is coming into agreement with God's opinion about our sins. Confession is looking at our sin through God's eyes and acknowledging that it is sin. Allow me to share a few examples of confession:

And Aaron said unto Moses, Alas, my lord, I beseech thee, lay not the sin upon us, wherein we have done foolishly, and wherein we have sinned (Numbers 12:11 KJV).

"All the people said to Samuel, 'Pray for your servants to the LORD your God, that we may not die, for we have added to all our sins this evil, to ask for ourselves a king'" (1 Samuel 12:19 ESV).

"But David's heart struck him after he had numbered the people. And David said to the Lord, 'I have sinned greatly in what I have done. But now, O Lord, please take away the iniquity of your servant, for I have done very foolishly'" (2 Samuel 24:10 KJV).

"Let thine ear now be attentive, and thine eyes open, that thou mayest hear the prayer of thy servant, which I pray before thee now, day and night, for the children of Israel thy servants, and confess the sins of the children of Israel, which we have sinned against thee: both I and my father's house have sinned. We have dealt very corruptly against thee, and have not kept the commandments, nor the statutes, nor the

28

judgments, which thou commandest thy servant Moses" (Nehemiah 1:6-7 KJV).

In each of these passages, and so many more, there is a clear recognition and acknowledgement of sin. There is no attempt to minimize, justify, or deflect blame to another. It is a person or a people who acknowledge that they have turned their backs on God, willfully disobeyed God, or perverted themselves in their open rebellion against God.

I am convinced beyond doubt that the clouds of the judgment of God are already gathering over the United States. We will soon be judged by the righteous hand of God for a multitude of sins—a judgment that will be terrible beyond what we can imagine. I also believe there is a way of escape—a way to stay the hand of God in executing His wrath. But first, we must come into agreement with God about our sin.

I understand the price that may be exacted from anyone who takes up the ministry of the watchman to warn the nation. Yet, God is calling forth in this hour a *watchman generation* that will need to endure the backdraft from an angry culture so that the blood of their destruction will not stain our hands. God never judges a nation without warning. Even if the nation refuses to heed the message, they can never say they have not heard. To the young man Jeremiah, the Lord spoke:

"The word of the Lord came to me a second time, saying, What do you see? And I said, I see a boiling pot, facing away from the north. Then the Lord said to me, Out of the north disaster shall be let loose upon all the inhabitants of the land. For behold, I am calling all the tribes of the kingdoms of the north, declares the Lord, and they shall come, and every one shall set his throne at the entrance of the gates of Jerusalem, against all its walls all around and against all the cities of Judah. And I will declare my judgments against them, for all their evil in forsaking me. They have made offerings to other gods and worshiped the works of their own hands. But you, dress yourself for work; arise, and say to them everything that I command you. Do not be dismayed by them, lest I dismay you before them. And I, behold, I make you this day a fortified city, an iron pillar, and bronze walls, against the whole land, against the kings of Judah, its officials, its priests, and the people of the land. They will fight against you, but they shall not prevail against you, for I am with you, declares the Lord, to deliver you." (Jeremiah 1:13-19 ESV)

As I read the words of God to Jeremiah, I grow increasingly concerned for our own nation. The sins of America so dangerously mirror the sins of ancient Israel. My prayer is that our response will not also mirror ancient Israel, who simply would not come into agreement with God.

"So you shall speak all these words to them, but they will not listen to you. You shall call to them, but they will not answer you. And you shall say to them, 'This is the nation that did not obey the voice of the Lord their God, and did not accept discipline; truth has perished; it is cut off from their lips'" (Jeremiah 7:27-28 ESV).

Not only Jeremiah, but prophet after prophet was sent from God to warn Israel of their impending destruction. They simply would not listen. They were righteous in their own eyes; they were secure in their own sight, and God's opinion simply did not matter to them. They would not listen, and they would not agree with God concerning their sins.

Like ancient Israel, our nation is not in agreement with God about our sins. There is a steady cry from politicians, from the media, and from Hollywood actors to rewrite the Bible. The Bible is out of date, archaic, and hateful. America is good in its own eyes. We have developed our own sense of right and wrong based upon our own perverted understanding of morality and justice. We are secure in our own devices. We believe the movie star. We believe the politician. We believe the false prophets, but we do not believe God, and we steadfastly refuse the message of His prophets.

The darkest day in Jeremiah's life came when God spoke in no uncertain terms to him concerning the fate of Israel: *"As for you, do not pray for this people, or lift up a cry or prayer for them, and do not intercede with me, for I will not hear you"* (Jeremiah 7:16 ESV).

Imagine the weight of those words upon Jeremiah's heart. Do not pray for this people, do not cry out for them, and do not intercede for them; I have already made up my mind.

I have not heard that command in my spirit, yet I live in dread of such a day. The only urging I have felt is to cry out to the church and to the nation, we must come into agreement with God regarding our sins. I'm getting to be an old man now, but I am praying that God will raise up a new generation of watchmen after the spirit of Jeremiah and Ezekiel. I pray for watchmen who possess spirits that are alive to the voice of God—watchmen who will not go the way of their peers but will stand apart. I pray they will stand when others kneel and will stand in the gap for the nation that God might not destroy it.

Men laughed at Noah as he labored to build the ark, preaching all the while that judgment was coming. God had not only commanded Noah to build this boat upon which his family and the animal kingdom would be delivered, He commanded Noah to warn the people that sudden destruction would befall them because of their sin. They laughed, they mocked, they called him a fool. But in one hour the biggest fool on the earth became the smartest guy in the room.

Part of the downfall of our nation must be laid at the feet of the church—that organism the Holy Spirit formed on the Day of Pentecost, birthed in the fires of adversity, and hardened through the rigors of persecution.

Living the life of ease and acceptance, the church has lost its metal. Instead of throwing ourselves across the destructive path of the culture, the church has chosen to merge into the flow of the world. We have become comfortable, complacent, and compromised. We have become enculturated.

The world has put its arm around the church and said, "Let's be buddies." Instead of being the voice of God to the culture, we have listened to the voice of men. We grow less and less godly and more and more worldly. We covet our 501c3 status more than we hunger for the Presence of God.

The church in America is an apostate church which in much the same way as the sinful Phineas and Hophni has caused people to despise the things of God. We have gorged ourselves on the best of the offerings, and we have compromised ourselves with the same lusts that motivate the world.

Rare is the ministry that knows how to love men in the world without becoming like men in the world. We have moderated our voice so that we might please men and in doing so, we have driven the Spirit of God from our midst.

Theologians in the church now sit in judgment of the Word of God providing a designer gospel wherein a man can enjoy fellowship with the church without being in fellowship with God. Instead of leaping into the arena of the world and shouting "STOP!" as did Telemachus, we have wallowed in the revelry of the world. Day by day the church looks less and less like the Bride of Christ and more and more like Hosea's whore. If our nation is ever going to come into agreement with God concerning our national sins, the church must first come into agreement with God concerning our own sins.

We need to name our sins. We need to be specific about our sins. And, we need to agree with God regarding our sin. While there are specific sins that are easily identified such as abortion, sexual perversion, pornography, and the destruction of the family, there are deeper, more critical heart issues that must be acknowledged if we are to come clean before God. In my book, *Cry Mercy*, I wrote the following:

For these reasons, my prayer is not for a Republican president but for a godly intercessor. I don't pray for a conservative Congress but for a humbled, broken and contrite representative government.

I do not pray that God (or anybody else) will make America great again. I do pray that God will

34

shatter our proud, arrogant American hearts that we might be ashamed before Him, that we might weep bitter tears of repentance as we are confronted with the enormity of our sin, and that the cry that would rise from our land would not be "God bless America," but "God forgive America."

God have mercy upon us and do not hold our sin against us. Preserve us by Your great grace; and give us new hearts, soft and humble in the place of our hard, arrogant, and wicked hearts. (Cry Mercy, Logos Publications, 2018, p 44).

I love America. I am blessed to have been born here and I wouldn't prefer to live anywhere else in the world. However, America is not a great nation. We were once a great nation that reverenced God, but we are now arrogant and proud and filled with iniquity. As such, we are facing the wrath of God.

I don't believe the Republican Party, Tea Party, or any other party can save America from the judgment of God because it's not our politics that need to be corrected, but our hearts. There are good people in America, but America is not good.

So many of my brothers and sisters in Christ have jumped on the Make America Great Again bandwagon, believing that conservative politics can somehow make us a good people again. We refuse to acknowledge that our country is rebellious against God and seeks only to do evil. We are, in many ways, like the church at Laodicea whom the Lord upbraided for their pride.

"For you say, I am rich, I have prospered, and I need nothing, not realizing that you are wretched, pitiable, poor, blind, and naked. I counsel you to buy from me gold refined by fire, so that you may be rich, and white garments so that you may clothe yourself and the shame of your nakedness may not be seen, and salve to anoint your eyes, so that you may see. Those whom I love, I reprove and discipline, so be zealous and repent" (Revelation 3:17-19 ESV).

We measure our morality by our prosperity, but we have forgotten that it was God that raised this nation up, blessed and enriched it—and it's God who can destroy it. As Israel was preparing to enter the Promised Land, God gave this dire warning to the nation through Moses:

"And when the Lord your God brings you into the land that he swore to your fathers, to Abraham, to Isaac, and to Jacob, to give you—with great and good cities that you did not build, and houses full of all good things that you did not fill, and cisterns that you did not dig, and vineyards and olive trees that you did not plant—and when you eat and are full, then take care lest you forget the Lord, who brought you out of the land of Egypt, out of the house of slavery. It is the Lord your God

36

you shall fear. Him you shall serve and by his name you shall swear. You shall not go after other gods, the gods of the peoples who are around you—for the Lord your God in your midst is a jealous God— lest the anger of the Lord your God be kindled against you, and he destroy you from off the face of the earth" (Deuteronomy 6:10-15 ESV).

We must agree with God concerning our Idolatry

God warned Israel against the sin of idolatry. He warned that if they should turn away from Him toward other gods, He would destroy them from off the face of the earth. Perhaps more than any other idol to which America has turned is the god of self. It would be difficult to argue that Americans are not self-absorbed, self-centered, self-indulgent, and self-promoting. Sadly, even the church is guilty of pandering to the self-consumed culture, emphasizing health, wealth, and happiness built upon the idol of self-esteem. Rather than being called to a specific church where we might be of service to the Body and to the world, we shop around for the church that best meets our perceived needs.

I hate abortion. I speak and write volumes about this heinous sin that has gripped our nation. Yet, as I have meditated on the various issues facing our nation, I have come to realize that abortion is the fruit, not the root. The sin of abortion is rooted in the idolatry of self. Abortion's primary justification is the right of a woman to her privacy. As a result, for any reason that a woman's "self" should choose ranging from her personal convenience, finances, her career, or even her personal beauty she can make the decision to take the life of her child. The banner defense of abortion is the preservation of a "woman's rights."

The rise of militant feminism and women's rights has become the fastest growing religion in America, and one of the primary gods of the new feminism is the god of death. Sadly, some of the priests of this new religion wear clerical robes, a collar around their neck, and a Bible under their arm as they sprinkle holy water in each surgical suite of abortion clinics around the nation and declare that abortion is a "gift from god," or "part of God's plan."

One such group, billed as an "interfaith gathering," the Ohio Religious Coalition for Reproductive Choice dedicated a new abortion clinic in Cleveland, Ohio by having a United Church of Christ minister on hand to bless the "sacred space of decision." [1]

We must come into agreement with God about our idolatry. Death has become an idol in the land which boasts of life, liberty, and the pursuit of happiness. Man has set himself up as the judge of who should or should not enjoy that pursuit.

In 2018, abortion became the leading cause of death worldwide with almost 42,000,000 abortions performed. Just shy of 1,000,000 of those abortions were performed in the United States. With increasing discussion regarding assisted suicide and euthanasia, the gods of death grow more powerful in our national consciousness every day.

We have established a macabre scale which we use to identify those who present an unnecessary drain on important resources—the unborn, the weak, and the old are seen as leeches who drain the resources of an ever self-consumed culture. God has warned, "whatsoever a man sows, that shall he reap." The generation that has aborted its children may be, in the end, aborted by its own children.

Along with our gods of money, power, and sex, this generation has bowed before the gods of death in an idolatry of blood-letting that will consume us as a people.

Consistent with many of the ancient cultic practices was sexual perversion, temple prostitution, pedophilia, and of course, child sacrifice. On the day the Judge Brett Kavanaugh hearings began, a replica of the ancient temple of Baal was erected on the Mall in Washington with a clear line of sight to the building where the hearings were being conducted. Witchcraft is active and growing in the land. Perhaps the most prominent idol of all in America is the god of Man himself. Humanism and science rule the nation as man has elevated himself as the supreme authority on all matters. We must agree with God that we are a nation of idol worshippers.

We must agree with God concerning our Pride and Arrogance

In 1715, King Louis XIV of France died after a reign of seventy-two years. He had called himself "the Great," and was the monarch who made the famous statement, "I am the state!" His court was the most magnificent in Europe, and his funeral was equally spectacular. As his body lay in state in a golden coffin, orders were given that the cathedral should be very dimly lit with only a special candle set above his coffin to dramatize his greatness. At the memorial, thousands waited in hushed silence. Then Bishop Massilon began to speak; slowly reaching down, he snuffed out the candle. As darkness engulfed the great cathedral, the Bishop's voice cut through the inky curtain, *"Only God is great."*

"Make America Great Again," suggests that America was once great. The truth is America is not great; America is blessed. She is rich. She has great power and influence, a military might second to none, technology that is the envy of the world, and natural resources and beauty that spans from one ocean to

40

another. Since the British were finally driven out, our people have never been subject to any government but our own. No war in the modern era has been waged on American soil, and our people have been blessed with more personal freedom and opportunity than any people in the history of civilization. These wonderful privileges do not mean that America is better than other nations. They are a testament to her blessings, not to her greatness.

Perhaps more than any nation on the earth, America represents the greatness of God. The psalmist has said, *"O Lord, not unto us, but unto thy name give glory, for thy mercy, and for thy truth's sake"* (Psalm 115:1 KJV) The height of pride is to take credit for what God has done. As a nation, America has been blessed by the hand of God in great measure, but we have come to believe that it is by our own hand that we have been lifted up.

"At the end of twelve months he was walking on the roof of the royal palace of Babylon, and the king answered and said, "Is not this great Babylon, which I have built by my mighty power as a royal residence and for the glory of my majesty?" (Daniel 4:29-30 ESV).

Nebuchadnezzar reigned over the greatest empire of history up until his time. Even though he had been warned by Daniel of his immense pride, he could not restrain himself from taking credit for all that he beheld from his balcony.

Even while his boastful words were in his mouth God spoke to him:

"O King Nebuchadnezzar, to you it is spoken: The kingdom has departed from you, and you shall be driven from among men, and your dwelling shall be with the beasts of field. And you shall be made to eat grass like and ox, and seven periods of time shall pass over you, until you know that the Most High rules the kingdom of men and gives it to whom he will" (Daniel 4:31-32 ESV).

America has removed God from the discussion as her leaders and people boast to the world, "Look what WE have built; look what WE have accomplished. WE are the greatest nation in the history of the earth!" I suspect it shall not be long before the Lord who raises up and brings down nations will lend His voice to the conversation, and the glory we believe to be ours, that we have earned will be taken from us.

The church does not get a pass on this point. Instead of running cross-culturally to that self-worship, the church has fed upon this pride and idolatry to enrich and empower itself. Speaking of the church in America, my good friend Paul Jehle of the Plymouth Rock Foundation says,

It is precisely because of this pervasive attitude of entitlement that comes from the root sin of pride that has caused us to act arrogant rather

than loving toward the culture we live in. We have become so self-absorbed in the righteousness that comes by our own effort (whether social or political) we virtually repel the very people we are praying to reach. We need a new dose of reality and God is faithful enough to bring this to His people through loving judgment. Judgment's purpose is redemptive, to "remember from whence you have fallen" and "repent."

I do understand that this is a broad-brush stroke and there certainly are many, many churches across the land who are faithfully preaching the Word of God. There are many pastors who have not capitulated to the pressure of the culture to conform to a more modern and enlightened theology. I celebrate these churches and their leaders. However, there are far too many churches who are silent on the sin of abortion and too frightened to speak God's mind on sexual perversion. There are too many denominations who claim to speak for God who are guilty of speaking for the god of this world, rather than the God of the Bible; too many hirelings who give power to the idolatry of this generation and too few shepherds who faithfully guard the sheep of God's pasture from error.

My cry to those churches who have abandoned their first love, *"Remember therefore from where you have fallen; repent and do the works you did at first. If not, I will come to you and remove your lampstand from its place, unless you repent."* (Revelation 2:5 ESV)

My plea to those churches that remain faithful to the truths of the Word of God is that they would not give up the fight for men's souls. Do not abandon the message of confession and repentance. Paul said, *"I am not ashamed of the gospel for it is the power of God unto salvation, to the Jew first and also the Greek."* (Romans 1:16 KJV)

There is no other message that will deliver men from the bondage of sin. There is no other message that will deliver our nation from our spiritual bondage. There is no other message that will dig down into the wicked soil of men's hearts and raise them up to new and transformed lives. And, there is no message more hated by a world driven by satanic powers.

The church that is embraced in America is the church that caters to the flesh rather than the spirit. A new breed of believers embraces any "faith" movement that promises health, wealth, or luxury. We run to the preacher who tells us that to follow Jesus is to become prosperous. We give in order to get. Instead of calling men into account for their avarice and self-seeking, the church has fed upon their pride and greed to amass great wealth for itself. The church is as the priests and prophets of Ezekiel who describes them: *"Her princes in her midst are like wolves tearing the prey, shedding blood, destroying lives to get dishonest gain. And her prophets have smeared whitewash for them, seeing false visions and divining lies for them, saying, 'Thus says the Lord God,' when the Lord has not spoken. The people of the land have practiced extortion and committed robbery. They have oppressed the poor and needy and have extorted from the sojourner without justice"* (Ezekiel 22:6-7).

America is guilty of many sins and it is vital that we come into agreement with God about those sins. Ironically, our most dangerous sin shields us from the humility that would cause us to bow before Him. It is our pride that is at the root of our rotting national tree.

We should note that the core of the movement that follows President Donald Trump is the *restoration of national pride*. The very thing that is rotting our national soul is the one thing that we seek the most. And that which we seek most earnestly is at the heart of our national downfall. *"God opposes the proud, but gives grace to the humble"* (James 4:6 ESV).

Let us carefully consider the warning to the Hebrews in Deuteronomy 8:

"Take care lest you forget the Lord your God by not keeping his commandments and his rules and his statutes, which I command you today, lest,

when you have eaten and are full and have built good houses and live in them, and when your herds and flocks multiply and your silver and gold is multiplied and all that you have is multiplied, then your heart be lifted up, and you forget the Lord your God, who brought you out of the land of Egypt, out of the house of slavery, who led you through the great and terrifying wilderness, with its fiery serpents and scorpions and thirsty ground where there was no water, who brought you water out of the flinty rock, who fed you in the wilderness with manna that your fathers did not know, that he might humble you and test you, to do you good in the end. Beware lest you say in your heart, 'My power and the might of my hand have gotten me this wealth.' You shall remember the Lord your God, for it is he who gives you power to get wealth, that he may confirm his covenant that he swore to your fathers, as it is this day. And if you forget the Lord your God and go after other gods and serve them and worship them, I solemnly warn you today that you shall surely perish. Like the nations that the Lord makes to perish before you, so shall you perish, because you would not obey the voice of the Lord your God" (Deuteronomy 8:11-20 ESV).

When asked whether he thought God was on the side of Union forces during the Civil War, Abraham Lincoln replied, *"Sir, my concern is not whether God is on our side; my greatest concern is to be on God's side, for God is always right."* (July 10, 1858, Lincoln's Senatorial Speech.)

America is no longer on God's side. We have chosen to stand on the side of the world, and friendship with the world is enmity with God. In other words, if we are not on God's side, then God is not on our side.

To find ourselves once again in the favor of God, we must abandon our pride and bow in humility before Him. We must cease being proud of our greatness and begin to be ashamed of our wickedness. It is fruitless to address issues such as abortion or sexual perversion until we address the underlying roots of our sin: Our pride, our arrogance, and our idolatry. We must agree with God that we are a prideful and arrogant people.

We must agree with God concerning our Lust and Sexual Perversion

America is a sexually driven culture. It would seem that sexuality has entwined itself into the very thought life of the nation. We are not just a sexually driven species; we are a sexually perverted species with a sexual appetite that cannot be sated. The culture has been locked in the grip of its sexually inflamed fantasies until it drives every facet of our lives. Our cars are sexy. We dress to be sexy. We search for pills and lotions that will make us more sexually potent or desirable.

Monogamy is a joke in this day of homosexual, bisexual, polyamorous, gender fluidity. Adultery and fornication are antiquated ideas of a sexually unenlightened bygone era. We are the "hook up" generation that has emerged as the result of the gross devaluation of sexual intimacy.

It is ironic that we live in a culture driven by sex, but an honest evaluation will reveal our sexuality has been stripped of any actual value beyond a series of hormonally driven interactions that demand no commitment, no responsibility, and are devoid of any intimacy. It's just biology. The idea of "cleaving" to one's wife and becoming "one flesh" has long time been degraded into a long series of bumping uglies whenever and with whomever, with little or no regard for love, commitment, or personal responsibility.

This sexual revolution has redefined the idea of relationships to hooking up, shacking up, and breaking up. There is nothing permanent, nothing stable, nothing fulfilling, nothing sacred, nothing endearing, nothing binding, and nothing intimate. It has promised satisfaction but, in the end, it has only created a greater and insatiable hunger.

This lust drive is destroying our humanity, degrading us to the level of instinct-driven animals on a never-ending quest for some kind of satisfaction. Because we cannot be truly satisfied by sex, the quest goes on and on, delving into more and more sexual activity—and perversion—in hopes that the next partner, the next sexual activity, the next orgasm, the next conquest will bring that for which we so greatly hunger. But there is a problem: We were not designed to be satisfied or fulfilled by sexual contact. We were created to find our satisfaction in God, in long term emotionally and spiritually satisfying relationships with a mate, and in all of the marvelous connotations that the idea of a mate brings with it.

This lustful spirit has driven us to sexualize our children at an increasingly young age as "sex education" is presented to ever younger children in an ever-increasing graphic detail. We are literally teaching our children the perversion our culture has been dragged into by its unsated lust. The lustful spirit that has gripped the heart of our nation is driving deeper and deeper, destroying everything that has value, even our own children. *"For all that is in the world, the lust of the flesh, and the lust of the eyes, and the pride of life, is not of the Father, but is of the world"* (1 John 2:16 KJV). We must come into agreement with God regarding our lust and sexual perversion.

If there is to be any hope for our nation, something has to drive us into agreement with God. This idea of agreeing with God could not be presented any more clearly than the apostle John does: *"If we confess our sins [agree with God], he is faithful and just to forgive us our sins and to cleanse us from all unrighteousness."*(1 John 1:9 ESV) John's "if" is a very important matter for he tells us that God's forgiveness is contingent upon our agreement with Him regarding our sins.

God pleads with Israel, *"Come now, and let us reason together, saith the Lord: though your sins be as scarlet, they shall be as white as snow; though they be red like crimson, they shall be as wool"* (Isaiah 1:18 KJV). For what purpose does God call us to "reason together" with Him if not that we would come into agreement? John and Isaiah agree that IF we will come into agreement with God concerning our sins, God has promised he will forgive our sins and cleanse us from the unrighteous stains that our sin has caused.

It is not only God's justice that drives His judgment, but His love. God loves us too much to allow us to continue in our sinful spiral away from Him. He will bring judgment as a tool to drive us back to Himself. If necessary, God will use His judgment to bring us into agreement with Him. The longer we take to turn, the longer and more entrenched we remain in our rebellion, the longer and more severe our judgment. The nation may not survive the judgment of God, but there will be men who will be driven to the Throne of God and personally redeemed. We must agree with God that we are a lustful and sexually perverted nation.

And yet, confession is not enough. Agreement with God regarding our sin is shallow and meaningless if it is not driven by genuine sorrow over our sin. Confession moves us toward repentance, but true repentance must be motivated by sincere sorrow or remorse for sin. It is more than being sorry that we got caught. There are many who are sorry in their sin but not for their sins. They are sorry for the consequences that have befallen them. They are sorry for the circumstances they are in. They are sorry for the trouble that has risen upon them because of their sin, but there is no acknowledgement that they have offended the heart of God. Their confession is woefully self-centered.

"I am sorry that I've lost my family because of my sin."

"I am sorry that I am broke and homeless because of my sin."

"I am sorry that I am sick, and ragged, and standing on a corner begging because of my sin."

"I'm not sorry that I sinned. I'm sorry for the trouble that my sin has caused me."

The focus of confession of a self-consumed generation is "I", *not God*. The focus is upon MY loss, MY trouble, MY suffering.

I have dealt with drunkards and addicts for years. I have heard the words, "I'm sorry," over and over again. Yet, for too many, it is not that they are sorry THAT they have sinned; they are sorry for the problems their sin has caused THEM.

Recently, I was in a conversation with my daughter-in-law in which she made a very astute observation, *"Dad, we have forgotten how to lament. We've lost the capacity to truly sorrow over our sin."* She is right on the money. Confession in the mind of most is limited to "Ah sorry, my bad."

Coming into agreement with God regarding our sin negates any blame transference or excuse making. The agreement God responds to is acknowledgement that I have acted wickedly, that I have acted selfishly. Read carefully the words of King David after being confronted by the prophet Nathan regarding his adultery with Bathsheba and the murder of her husband:

Have mercy on me, O God,
according to your steadfast love;
according to your abundant mercy
blot out my transgressions.
Wash me thoroughly from my iniquity,
and cleanse me from my sin!
For I know my transgressions,
and my sin is ever before me.
Against you, you only, have I sinned
and done what is evil in your sight,

so that you may be justified in your words
and blameless in your judgment.
Behold, I was brought forth in iniquity,
and in sin did my mother conceive me.
Behold, you delight in truth in the inward being,
and you teach me wisdom in the secret heart.
Purge me with hyssop, and I shall be clean;
wash me, and I shall be whiter than snow.
Let me hear joy and gladness;
let the bones that you have broken rejoice.
Hide your face from my sins,
and blot out all my iniquities.
Create in me a clean heart, O God,
and renew a right spirit within me.
Cast me not away from your presence,
and take not your Holy Spirit from me.
Restore to me the joy of your salvation,
and uphold me with a willing spirit.
Then I will teach transgressors your ways,
and sinners will return to you.
Deliver me from bloodguiltiness, O God,
O God of my salvation,
and my tongue will sing aloud of your
righteousness.
O Lord, open my lips,
and my mouth will declare your praise.
For you will not delight in sacrifice, or I would
give it;
you will not be pleased with a burnt offering.
The sacrifices of God are a broken spirit;

a broken and contrite heart, O God, you will not despise.

(Psalm 51:1-17 ESV)

David's confession is genuine. He does not make excuses, and he makes no effort to shift blame. (*The woman shouldn't have been bathing on her rooftop. It's her fault for tempting me.*) David's heart is broken because of his sin and his plea is contrite. He acknowledges that his sin is, first of all, against God.

In Luke 15 we find a young man sitting in pig slop, waiting for the pigs to finish eating so that he might eat from the same slop trough. Because of his own selfish decisions, he finds himself completely destitute and without any help from anyone. He had demanded his share of the inheritance of his father, abandoned the family business, and wasted the fruit of his father's labors on what the Bible calls "riotous living." When he had spent it all and had nothing left, he hired himself out to feed pigs so that he might have something, however revolting, to eat. He was a broken, ruined man.

"But when he came to himself, he said, 'How many of my father's hired servants have more than enough bread, but I perish here with hunger! I will arise and go to my father, and I will say to him, "Father, I have sinned against heaven and before you. I am no longer worthy to be called your son.

Treat me as one of your hired servants." (Luke 15:17-19 ESV)

The young man dragged himself out of the pig slop and headed home. When he was still some distance away, his father saw him and ran to him, throwing his arms around him and welcomed him home. An important thing to note here is that the father did not go after his son. He did not try to rescue him from his trouble, and he did not make the first move. He waited. He waited until his boy had *come to himself.* Any rescue would have been wasted if the boy was not ready for change. But there was a change on the inside—a broken, contrite, sorrowful spirit that cried out for mercy. When the cry for help came, the father was ready and willing. No, more...he was *anxious* to bring him back into the house.

"Yet even now," declares the Lord, *"return to me with all your heart, with fasting, with weeping, and with mourning; and rend your hearts and not your garments." Return to the Lord your God, for he is gracious and merciful, slow to anger, and abounding in steadfast love; and he relents over disaster"* (Joel 2:12-13 ESV).

"But the tax collector, standing far off, would not even lift up his eyes to heaven, but beat his breast, saying, 'God, be merciful to me, a sinner!'" (Luke 18:13 ESV).

"Draw near to God, and he will draw near to you. Cleanse your hands, you sinners, and purify your hearts, you double-minded. Be wretched and mourn and weep. Let your laughter be turned to mourning and your joy to gloom. Humble yourselves before the Lord, and he will exalt you" (James 4:8-10 ESV).

"For godly grief produces a repentance that leads to salvation without regret, whereas worldly grief produces death" (2 Corinthians 7:10 ESV).

There is a familiar theme to each of these Scriptures: *We have to make the first move.* God will not deliver us from the pig slop of our lives until we WANT to be delivered from the pig slop of our lives. In the story of the prodigal and in each of the verses above the sinner makes the first move. Return to me, draw near to me, purify your heart, humble yourselves.

The message is consistent and clear. If you are wallowing in the pig slop of this life, abandoned and used up by all of your partying friends, your money wasted and gone, destitute and hopeless, do not expect your Heavenly Father to come get you. But, if you will come to your senses and take one step away from your rebellion, He will come running to you, wrap His arms around you, wash away your sins in the blood of His own Son, and welcome you home.

Before a man will change his life, he must decide to change (repent). What drives a man to change, is a recognition that he is guilty. Because he recognizes he is guilty and is sincerely sorry for what he has done, he repents. It is an ancient biblical pattern that has been repeated over and over again; a pattern that according to the Scriptures is an absolutely necessary pattern for receiving forgiveness of sin. Confessing leads to lamenting which leads to repenting. But there is a problem: *America is not in agreement with God*

The grave peril in which America finds itself is that as a nation we are not in agreement with God about our sin. In fact, we celebrate our sins.

America is in open rebellion against the decrees of God. We do not acknowledge God's authority in our national life at any level. We have declared that separation of Church and State means that God has nothing to do with our conduct as a people. Those who do bring God into the discussion have so twisted the Word of God as to say He not only allows our behavior, but in fact, fully encourages our perversion.

We encourage one another in our sins. We help men to continue in sin. We legislate to protect sinners. We prefer sin over righteousness. We celebrate the sinner and prosecute the righteous. *"They know God's decree, that those who practice such things deserve to die—yet they not only do them but even applaud others who practice them"* (Romans 1:32 NSRV).

We have lost the capacity for sorrow over sin. The pig slop in which America wallows today is getting deeper and deeper and more disgusting every day, and we are yet to come to the end of ourselves.

The judgment of God is never more vivid than when He simply allows us to continue in our rebellion, giving us up to our reprobate minds, allowing us to reap the consequences of our sin. As men, as a nation, we have forgotten that sin itself bears its own judgment. God is not required to do anything except to not save us from ourselves. We cannot fix ourselves, but we can certainly destroy ourselves.

I stood beside the bedside of a young man who was very ill, near death even. He looked me in the eye and said these words, *"Pastor, I am simply reaping the harvest of my own wild oats."* That young man realized that God was not punishing him for his sin, but simply allowing the harvest of his sin to spring up.

America is reaping a harvest of the "wild oats" we've been sowing for the past few generations. It is not that God is unleashing judgment upon us, but our own sin is yielding its crop. Paul says, "for this reason, God gave them over to a reprobate mind." (Romans 1:28 KJV) Our passion for self-fulfillment has brought us to the pig pen in which we sit today.

We have so many "social" problems in a generation of young adults who have shunned education in favor of the party, abandoned purity for sexual license, and who have chosen a perpetual, drug-fueled euphoria in favor of personal responsibility. I see them, every day, standing on street corners, at mall entrances, and doorways along the street holding cardboard signs with scribbled words, "Homeless, any act of kindness will help." They burglarize, steal from one another, shoplift, and beg just to survive, all the while blaming the government for not giving them enough of what men at one time felt the responsibility to earn.

This is not God judging America. It is America reaping the harvest of its own wild oats. We are not sorry; *we are mad!* We're mad at the government, mad at the rich, mad at the police, mad at the president (doesn't matter which one), and we're mad at God. We're mad because we have discovered that wild oat seed produces weeds and not wheat.

If the government was good, it would give me all the things I need.

If the people on the streets were good, they would toss money in my hat.

If God was good, He wouldn't let me be in this situation. A good God wouldn't let me go hungry and be homeless and sick.

If God were real and if God were good, He would fix this mess. Why would a good God not prevent the murder of innocent children by a crazy man in their school? Why won't God protect us from terrorists?

We are not in agreement with God about our sin. It must be the government; we have to change the government. It must be the rich; we have to punish the rich. It must be God. Surely, He is not a good God, or He would do something. We are sitting in the pig slop of our lives, broken and confused. We don't know how we got here, and we don't know how to get out of here. We do not understand why things are so bad and we blame God.   It's not God—it is us. We have sown to the wind and now we are reaping the whirlwind.

[1](https://www1.cbn.com/cbnnews/us/2018/october/like-priests-standing-outside-the-gas-chambers-at-auschwitz-religious-leaders-bless-abortion-clinic-as-sacred-space)

4 | Repentance

John, the cousin of Jesus, came roaring out of the wilderness with a single message--Repent! Given his living arrangements, John's appearance could scarcely have been much better than that of Jonah as he walked through the gates of Nineveh. His message was even more direct than that of Jonah. It was simply, "Repent."

When John called for the people to repent, he was not referring to some mere academic change of mind, nor simply regret or remorse. The repentance John called for represented a radical turning from sin. His repentance involved more than repeating a "sinner's prayer," or filling out a decision card.

Repentance is the sister to confession. They are twins, joined at the hip so to speak. One is meaningless without the other. Confession is coming into agreement with God, but confession must be wed to repentance. Repentance requires a change of direction. Repentance requires an abandonment of sin. Repentance means to convert, to turn, to abandon the wickedness about which we have come into agreement with God.

In one of the most famous Bible verses concerning repentance we read this powerful truth: *"If my people who are called by my name humble themselves [pride], and pray and seek my face [idolatry] and turn from their wicked ways [repentance], then I will hear from heaven and will forgive their sin and heal their land"* (2 Chronicles 7:14 ESV Brackets mine).

There is an open invitation here from God to a rebellious people filled with pride, sold out to idolatry, and steeped in wickedness to repent.

In the story of the Prodigal Son in Luke 15, there was a moment when he was sorry. That sorrow led him to a moment of repentance. He stood up, climbed over the fence of the pigsty, and turned toward home.

Repentance is not coming to an altar.

Repentance is not filling out a decision card.

Repentance is not attending church services.

Repentance is turning from the sin that has separated you from God and His blessings.

"From that time Jesus began to preach his message: Turn away from your sins [repent], because the Kingdom of heaven is near!" (Matthew 4:17 TEV).

"Repent, then, and turn to God, so that he will forgive your sins" (Acts 3:19 TEV).

"Let him that stole steal no more: but rather let him labour, working with his hands the thing which is good, that he may have to give to him that needeth" (Ephesians 4:28 KJV).

The thief will stop stealing. The liar will turn to the truth. The drunkard will sober up. We are not able to do any of these things on our own, but we can turn our hearts toward God and ask for His help. If a man says he has repented but continues in his sins, he has not repented. His heart has not turned.

Repentance is more about a change of heart than a change in behavior, but repentance always leads to a change in behavior. A man who truly repents will change. He will turn. He will cease his rebellion. When I was a young man, an elderly man in my church was fond of the saying, *"If nothing happens, then nothing happened."*

"If we say that we have fellowship with him, and walk in darkness, we lie, and do not the truth" (1 John 1:6 KJV). In other words, if we continue in our rebellion, we have not repented. This is not self-righteousness, or legalism, or works-based salvation. *This is common sense.*

No one of us can escape the clutches of sin in our lives without the help of the Holy Spirit, without the washing of the Word of God to renew our minds. We cannot purify ourselves. We are purified only by the blood of Christ. However, repentance represents a change of mind about our sin and a change of heart regarding our desires.

We are called upon to show the "fruits" of repentance. Will the repentant man commit sins? Of course he will, because we are all still at war with our flesh and our flesh is weak. But the truly repentant grieves over his sins. He confesses (agrees with God) that he has sinned, and faithfully seeks forgiveness for his sins. His heart is turned toward God and His righteousness. Change in behavior is not a requirement for salvation, but it is the evidence of repentance.

Nations don't repent—men repent.

America must repent. We must come into agreement with God about our grave national sins and turn from them. However, governments don't repent. A nation cannot turn away from or back to God. Nations don't have hearts and minds that can be changed.

Daniel fell into his room with a heavy heart and flung open the window facing Jerusalem. He was a righteous man among the heathen. He had a pure heart and uncompromised life. Daniel had been faithful to God, risking his life rather than compromise godly principles learned in his youth.

And yet, hear him pray! His mournful groans could be heard by passersby as he hefted the weight of the sins of the nation upon his own shoulders and cried out to the God of Abraham, Isaac, and Jacob.

"Ah, Lord, great and awesome God, keeping covenant and steadfast love with those who love you and keep your commandments, we have sinned and done wrong, acted wickedly and rebelled, turning aside from your commandments and ordinances. We have not listened to your servants the prophets, who spoke in your name to our kings, our princes, and our ancestors, and to all the people of the land.

"Righteousness is on your side, O Lord, but open shame, as at this day, falls on us, the people of Judah, the inhabitants of Jerusalem, and all Israel, those who are near and those who are far away, in all the lands to which you have driven them, because of the treachery that they have committed against you. Open shame, O Lord, falls on us, our kings, our officials, and our ancestors, because we have sinned against you. To the Lord our God belong mercy and forgiveness, for we have rebelled against him, and have not obeyed the voice of the Lord our God by following his laws, which he set before us by his servants the prophets.

"All Israel has transgressed your law and turned aside, refusing to obey your voice. So, the curse and the oath written in the law of Moses, the

servant of God. have been poured out upon us, because we have sinned against you" (Daniel 9:4-11 NRSV).

When Daniel prayed, he was repenting for the sins of his people. He was standing in the gap for them. There was no "nation" of Israel; *not anymore.* Israel lay in ruin, its capital city crushed to dust, its temple pulled down to the ground. Daniel is not confessing the sins of the government, He is confessing the sins of the people—all of them, starting with the kings down to each and every member of the society.

Daniel is not confessing a political failure, but the *moral failure* of all of the people. His heart was broken for the people. In Daniel's mind, Israel was so much more than a piece of real estate. Israel was a promise; a prophetic key to the redemption of all the nations. Daniel not only longed for God's people to return to Jerusalem, he longed for them to return to God.

I confess to a recurring vision of one day tuning my television to C-SPAN to find every member of our Congress on their faces, weeping before God and confessing their sins, crying out to God that He might have mercy upon the land. Instead of a great rally on the Mall in Washington, protesting this or that the government has done or is doing or is thinking about doing, I dream of a great revival sweeping across the nation bringing us all to our knees in a great wave of confession and repentance. Ours is not a failure of government. It is a moral failure that goes to the very root of who we are as a people.

The people of Israel did repent, but not until 70 years of exile in Persia had completely crushed and broken the people did it come to pass. God will allow the weight of our sin to bear down upon us until we are completely broken beneath its awful burden. When we can no longer bear it, we might cry out to Him for mercy.

I hear many moan about their perception of injustice from God. Why is He doing these terrible things to our land? Why does He not intervene? If God is so good, how can he allow so much suffering into the world? The more I meditate on these things the clearer it becomes. God is not doing anything to America. He is simply allowing us to reap the harvest of our own sin. We are living in a hell of our own making.

Sin brings a terrible weight to bear, and the more we persist in our sin, the more crushing is the weight of it. It is not the hand of God that is bearing down on us but the weight of our own iniquity. Only God can deliver us from that awful burden, but in order for that to happen we must turn to Him with a broken and contrite spirit and cry out for help. Like the father longing for the return of the Prodigal our Father waits. He waits while the consequences of our sin take their full toll. He waits even while the savagery of our own sins tears us and brings us to ruin.

We love to quote: *"For surely I know the plans I have for you, says the Lord, plans for your welfare and not for harm, to give you a future with hope"* (Jeremiah 29:11 NSRV). This is a beautiful verse, and we love to quote it. We buy it on plaques and hang it in our kitchen. It is printed on bookmarks in our Bibles. However, most of us do not understand the context in which this verse is written. This promise was given to a people who had been dragged off into slavery. They would live for 70 years, first under the heel of Nebuchadnezzar and then Cyrus and Darius. They would be slaves to another kingdom until their hearts were crushed and they would cry out to God. In this context God says, "I have plans for you—good plans for you, and your exile is a critical part of those plans."

How long will we persist in our rebellion against God? How long will we live in servitude to another kingdom? How long will we bend beneath the weight of our national sin before we repent of our sins and cry out for mercy? How much suffering will we endure before we yield to His grace? I don't know, but I am confident He will not rescue us until we come to ourselves and ask for His help in crawling out of the pigsty we have built for ourselves. He will sit on the porch of our homestead, longing and looking, and waiting.

My heart is drawn back to the Book of Ezekiel in the Old Testament where, through the prophet, God pronounces judgment upon the nation of Israel. In this passage, Ezekiel highlights four classes of people who have set the nation up for judgment. He specifically mentions prophets, priests, politicians, and the people. God declares that He has sought for someone among the prophets, the priests, and the politicians to stand in the gap before Him, to plead for the lives of this wicked people who have turned their backs upon Him, who have fallen into a sexual frenzy, and who regularly spill innocent blood. In all the land, God could not find a man who would stand in the gap.

The prophets had failed to bring a true word of warning to the people. In fact, they had become a protective shield for the wickedness of government. The princes (politicians) preyed upon the weak like ravenous wolves. The priests profaned the things of God so that the people could no longer distinguish between that which is holy and that which is profane. They called evil good and good evil. They enriched themselves upon the offerings of the poor and needy while ignoring the needs of the lowliest of the people. The people abused, extorted, cheated, and robbed one another.

As I have read and re-read this passage in several translations and paraphrases, I keep thinking, *Welcome to America!*

I am not a huge fan of The Message paraphrase. However, as I was reading through the 22nd chapter of Ezekiel in several different versions, I was especially taken by The Message's version of this prophecy from Ezekiel. Take note of how many times God refers to idols, the shedding of innocent blood, unrestrained sexual perversion, and sexual violence. *(Please read the following verses entirely – do not skip over them as if they were not important to this message.)*

God's Message came to me: "Son of man, are you going to judge this bloody city or not? Come now, are you going to judge her? Do it! Face her with all her outrageous obscenities. Tell her, 'This is what God, the Master, says: You're a city murderous at the core, just asking for punishment. You're a city obsessed with no-god idols, making yourself filthy. In all your killing, you've piled up guilt. In all your idol-making, you've become filthy. You've forced a premature end to your existence. I'll put you on exhibit as the scarecrow of the nations, the world's worst joke. From far and near they'll deride you as infamous in filth, notorious for chaos.

"'Your leaders [politicians], the princes of Israel among you, compete in crime. You're a

community that's insolent to parents, abusive to outsiders, oppressive against orphans and widows. You treat my holy things with contempt and desecrate my Sabbaths. You have people spreading lies and spilling blood, flocking to the hills to the sex shrines and fornicating unrestrained. Incest is common. Men force themselves on women regardless of whether they're ready or willing. Sex is now anarchy. Anyone is fair game: neighbor, daughter-in-law, sister. Murder is for hire, usury is rampant, extortion is commonplace.

"'And you've forgotten me. Decree of God, the Master.

"'Now look! I've clapped my hands, calling everyone's attention to your rapacious greed and your bloody brutalities. Can you stick with it? Will you be able to keep at this once I start dealing with you?

"'I, God, have spoken. I'll put an end to this. I'll throw you to the four winds. I'll scatter you all over the world. I'll put a full stop to your filthy living. You will be defiled, spattered with your own mud in the eyes of the nations. And you'll recognize that I am God.'"

God's Message came to me: "Son of man, the people of Israel are slag to me, the useless byproduct of refined copper, tin, iron, and lead left at the smelter—a worthless slag heap. So tell them, 'God, the Master, has spoken: Because you've all become worthless slag, you're on notice: I'll assemble you in Jerusalem. As men gather silver, copper, iron, lead, and tin into a furnace and blow fire on it to melt it down, so in my wrath I'll gather you and melt you down. I'll blow on you with the fire of my wrath to melt you down in the furnace. As silver is melted down, you'll be melted down. That should get through to you. Then you'll recognize that I, God, have let my wrath loose on you.'"

God's Message came to me: "Son of man, tell her, 'You're a land that during the time I was angry with you got no rain, not so much as a spring shower. The leaders among you became desperate, like roaring, ravaging lions killing indiscriminately. They grabbed and looted, leaving widows in their wake.

"'Your priests [preachers] violated my law and desecrated my holy things. They can't tell the difference between sacred and secular. They tell people there's no difference between right and wrong. They're contemptuous of my holy Sabbaths, profaning me by trying to pull me down to their level. Your politicians are like wolves prowling and killing and rapaciously taking whatever they want. Your preachers cover up for the politicians by pretending to have received *visions and special revelations. They say, "This is what God, the Master, says . . ." when God hasn't said so much as one word. Extortion is rife, robbery is epidemic, the poor and needy are abused, outsiders are kicked around at will, with no access to justice.'*

"I looked for someone to stand up for me against all this, to repair the defenses of the city, to take a stand for me and stand in the gap to protect this land so I wouldn't have to destroy it. I couldn't find anyone. Not one. So I'll empty out my wrath on them, burn them to a crisp with my hot anger, serve them with the consequences of all they've done. Decree of God, the Master" (Ezekiel 22:1–31 MSG).

I have read so many prophetic declarations recently, promising a great day of revival in America. They declare that Donald Trump will protect religious freedom and the church will be delivered from persecution by his administration. The Lord will pour out His Spirit upon the land and a great revival will flow from sea to shining sea.

The message I am not hearing though, is the message of confession and repentance. I suppose we will wallow in our pig slop until the Father grows weary of waiting and will come to rescue us, pouring out His blessings upon a spiritually dull, unrepentant nation. This goes against everything the Bible teaches us.

"If we confess our sins, [then] he is faithful and just to forgive us our sins and to cleanse us from all unrighteousness. (1 John 1:9 ESV emphasis added).

This is a powerful promise, but it is a *conditional* promise. There is a huge "IF" that cannot be ignored. That same conditional promise is found in (2 Chronicles 7:14 ESV): "IF my people who are called by my name humble themselves, and pray and seek my face and turn from their wicked ways, THEN I will hear from heaven and will forgive their sin and heal their land" (emphasis added).

These are conditional promises which include an if/then clause. The first move (the "if") is ours, not God's. He will move IF we will confess and repent of our sins. He will forgive and heal IF we will turn to Him and repent of our evil. Until then, our Father waits ... He patiently waits. If we do not turn, if we do not come into agreement with Him regarding our sins, and if we do not repent and turn away from our evil, then we will be ultimately crushed under the weight of our own rebellion and lost to the wonderful promises God has made to us.

5 | Time to Decide

"I call heaven and earth to witness against you today, that I have set before you life and death, blessing and curse. Therefore choose life, that you and your offspring may live" (Deuteronomy 30:19 ESV).

The United States of America is at a crossroads. Our nation faces a far greater decision than a choice between capitalism or socialism, conservative or progressive, Republican or Democrat. We stand at the junction of survival and desolation. God has put the ball in our court, so to speak. We have the power to choose whether we will be the recipients of His continued benevolence or whether we will feel the wrath of His judgment. Our collective decision hinges on a single issue; obedience or continued rebellion.

"See, I am setting before you today a blessing and a curse: the blessing, if you obey the commandments of the Lord your God, which I command you today, and the curse, if you do not obey the commandments of the Lord your God, but turn aside from the way that I am commanding

you today, to go after other gods that you have not known" (Deuteronomy 11:26–28 ESV).

But, it is not for the United States of America to repent. A government can neither rebel nor repent. Real estate set apart by geographic boundaries does not have a heart, a mind, or a conscience. When we call upon any nation to repent, we are calling upon the men and women who live within those borders to repent. There is an appeal to those who hold offices within that government to repent of their personal and corporate sins, and having repented, to show the fruit of their repentance by enacting legislation in keeping with the laws of God.

As they laid the foundations of the nation, our founders entered into covenants with the God of Abraham, Isaac, and Jacob. In his inaugural address our first President, George Washington, spoke these powerful words:

"Since we ought to be no less persuaded that the propitious smiles of Heaven, can never be expected on a nation that disregards the eternal rules of order and right, which Heaven itself has ordained: And since the preservation of the sacred fire of liberty, and the destiny of the Republican model of Government, are justly considered as deeply, perhaps as finally staked, on the experiment entrusted to the hands of the American people."

Washington could not have been clearer: No nation should expect the blessings of God should they turn away from Him and reject His *eternal rules of order and right.* The nation that turns away from God will surely lose the blessings He has bestowed upon her.

Upon taking the oath of office, Washington became the federal head of the United States of America, and as such he entered into a covenant with God. This covenant was not made with some "higher power" or an unknowable theistic force of the universe. He entered into covenant with the God of the Bible—the God of Abraham, Isaac, and Jacob. Washington entered into a covenant on behalf of the nation that America would follow God. That covenant, made with the agreement of the Congress, stipulated that should America turn from God America would lose His favor and blessings. Washington was sure God would keep His promise. God always keeps His promises. The greater issue is this: Would America honor the covenant as well?

America has not kept the covenant, and as a result America has forfeited the blessings of that covenant. One piece of shocking evidence of this forfeiture was delivered to our shores early on the morning of September 11, 2001, when for the first time since the Revolution, America was successfully attacked by the enemies from which God had so long protected her.

Politicians in Washington, as well as at state and local levels, are moving America further and further away from that covenant. We have not simply forgotten God; we have tried to kick God out of office. We have foolishly, even wickedly, thought we could impeach God, and America is paying the price of that disastrous delusion. Despite every malicious attempt to marginalize godly influence, God is still on the Throne of the Universe. And despite our prideful national confidence, we cannot sustain our nation apart from the favor and protection of God.

Josiah became king over Israel at the tender age of eight years old after his father had been assassinated in 604 B.C. He reigned for 34 years and was instrumental in bringing the people of Israel to a renewed relationship with God. He was responsible for closing down pagan worship sites and practices and restoring Davidic worship to the temple. My friend John Goyette says in his book, *The Power of Return*, that every spiritual renewal in Biblical history is marked by the rise of strong, godly leadership.

There is open warfare in Washington right now. We can see the political warfare, but most are not aware of the warfare in the shadows, in the spiritual, unseen realm. It is not a warfare between Republicans and Democrats—it is a war waged with powers and principalities, spiritual wickedness in high places. It is a warfare for the soul of America, and it troubles me that so many within the church somehow feel that this warfare can be won in the political arena. It cannot be won through elections and legislation. This war must be won on our knees using spiritual, not carnal, weapons of warfare.

We need a strong, godly leader who walks in the anointing of God, who is fearless before the enemies of God, and who will set his face like a flint to the restoration of America to the covenants of God established by our founders. This type of leader cannot be merely elected; he must be raised up by the Hand of God Himself. This one will come only through much prayer and fasting.

America has abandoned our covenant with God and America needs a Josiah.

The church in America is at a crossroads. We can show the way by confession and repentance from our own sins which are far greater than we would care to admit. However, the church as an institution cannot repent. Institutions do not repent, people repent. As with America, the church needs strong, godly leadership to rise up in this generation to pull us back from the brink of complete apostasy. In fact, much of what we see in

America is not the church; it is not the Bride of Christ. There is a religious whore passing herself off as the church.

The apostasy of the church deepens as wolves roam around dressed in priestly vestments while daring to say they speak for God as they cunningly lead witless sheep into perdition. Under the banner of *"God is Still Speaking,"* they declare that God speaks differently now than He once did. The God of the 21st century is nicer, kinder, more tolerant, universally accepting. There is no blood, no cross, no confession of sin, no repentance needed; and absolutely no judgment.

Church councils sit in judgment of the Word of God, declaring His verdicts to be unreasonable and invalid in today's enlightened society. Men and women in clerical garb walk through abortion clinics, sprinkling "holy water" to bless torture chambers where the innocent are heartlessly ripped in pieces from their mother's womb and declaring abortion to be God's work.

Those deceivers must be named for who they are and identified for what they are. Of course, anyone who exposes the false prophet is called divisive and hateful, destroying the unity of the church, as if these soothsayers were ever an actual part of the church. They are not, and all true believers must separate themselves from them. Leaders in the Body of Christ must repent of our cowardice as we have allowed ravenous wolves to ravage and destroy lives in the name of God.

We must repent of our tepid defense of biblical principles and a spiritual lifestyle. Jesus said to the church at Laodicea, *"I know your works: you are neither cold nor hot. Would that you were either cold or hot! So, because you are lukewarm, and neither hot nor cold, I will spit you out of my mouth"* (Revelation 3:15–16 ESV).

False teachers have systematically reduced the Word of God to a collection of fables, stories, and platitudes; principles suggested, but not commanded, as we have stood by while the justice of God has been subjugated to the love of God and the Lion of the Tribe of Judah has been reduced in the eyes of men to little more than a pussycat.

Pulpits have been bullied into silence—no, even compliance—by feminist, LBGTQ, and pro-abortion activists under threat of harassment and prosecution. The message of the modern church has abandoned transformation of the spirit in favor of affirmation of the flesh.

While we are commanded to love all persons, compassionately serve the communities we live in, and seek justice and mercy for all men, saint and sinner alike, we do disservice to the gospel and dishonor Christ when in His name, we celebrate and encourage men in their rebellion.

Our mission is to call all men to repentance, to plead with them to turn from their sin and be saved, to save themselves from a crooked and perverse generation by calling upon His name and abandoning their wicked lives in favor of the life of Christ.

At all cost, our message must be one of confession and repentance of sin, and as the Day of His Appearing draws closer, our sense of urgency toward that message must grow. At all cost, by all means, to martyrdom, if need be, the church must find its voice again to call men to the cross.

Remove the cowards from the pulpit, the compromisers, the con men, and the flesh peddlers. We need warriors, we need giant slayers, we need men who will grab the wolf by the beard and who will drive away the thief. The pulpit must stop bending to the voice of the sheep and begin again to listen for the voice of the Master.

There is no need to apologize for the severity of Scriptures regarding the condition of a man's heart. There is no need to attempt to "make God nicer," for God is not nice. God is good, but He is not nice. God is compassionate, but He is not permissive. God is approachable, but He is not common. God is not our buddy. He is the Great God, the Ancient of Days, the Potentate who sits upon the Throne of the Universe. The stars compose His crown and the planets His footstool.

It is utterly right that we should stand in abject awe and utter terror. He is the Mighty One of Israel before whom men ought to tremble and bow, to plead rather than demand, to revere in the knowledge that it is He who can blot out our name from the Book of Life. Oh, but only for the Incarnation of Christ can we know His compassion and mercy and forgiveness. We must see His majesty before we can comprehend our desperate depravity. Like Isaiah, we must see him high and lifted up before our wicked hearts can truly bow and truly repent. Men can no longer distinguish between the holy and the profane because the god we have preached has become so utterly . . . *human.*

When you castrate a bull, he can pull the plow, but he can no longer produce life. When we remove or reduce the message of confession and repentance, we neuter the pulpit. It can conduct meetings and take offerings; it can impress by its oratory and titillate through its cleverness—but that pulpit cannot produce life. It can excite, it can entertain, it can produce great television. That pulpit can even produce tears, but it cannot produce life. Without the message of repentance there is no gospel, there is no good news, there is no transformation. It is the same old life dressed up in fancy new clothes, but dressed without the washing, without the cleansing, and without the aroma of Christ.

The church must repent of preaching a Christ that lives only to give us things—a Christ that exists to bless us, to heal us, and to deliver us. We have presented a Christ to the world that is for us. The truth is that we were made for Him. We were made by Him for Him for His own glory. He is the center and the universe that revolves around Him. He is preeminent in all things. When we live only for ourselves, we do not comprehend Christ and we are in rebellion.

The church must decide whether it serves Christ or man. If our decision is that we serve Christ, then we must bring the message of Christ to men. When Jesus returned from the wilderness and His confrontation with Satan, he began from that day to declare, "Repent for the Kingdom of Heaven is at hand." Jesus came to reconcile us to the Father. He came to restore that fellowship that was destroyed by sin in the Garden of Eden. Jesus came to break the bondage of sin that holds each of us captive until we confess our sinful helplessness and repent so that we might have the power to become sons of God.

We have falsely taught that we are all God's children. We are not. The right to become sons of God is reserved for those who receive Him, and the only way to receive Christ is through confession and repentance. I am not a son of God because I was born of a woman. I am a son of God because I was born of the Spirit and cleansed of my sins by the shed blood of Jesus Christ. I only have access to that cleansing forgiveness through confession and repentance. Until that transaction takes place, I am not a son of God, but a son of the devil, and I must look toward judgment with terror and dread.

Every man, woman, and child in America is at a crossroads. We are at a crossroads because institutions cannot repent. Governments cannot repent. Nations cannot repent. Churches cannot repent. It is men that must repent.

We are in desperate need of a heaven borne wind of conviction which causes men to look upon their sinful state and cry out to God with a desperate plea for forgiveness. We must repent for abortion. We must repent of our sexual perversion and of our greed, our injustice, our racism, and our idolatry. We must mourn the death of 60,000,000 innocent children. As men and women, we must mourn the disintegration of our families, the defilement of our marriages, and the corruption of generation after generation of our children.

May God break our hearts. May He remove the spiritual blindness that hides our sin from us in a grand delusion of self-righteousness. May God break the granite of our hardened hearts that has left us cold and calloused, no longer able to feel the weight of our wickedness. This conviction cannot be accomplished by a book, a sermon, or laws. This kind of spiritual awakening must originate from the heavens, and we must pray zealously for a move of God that will shatter our pride and arrogance. We must cry out for a move of God that will strip us naked of any hope that we can save ourselves, leaving us broken and ashamed and helpless. The message of the church, yes, every man and woman in the church, must be *Repent, for the Kingdom of Heaven is at Hand*. That was the message of Christ and so it ought also to be ours. Our message is not, "Come to our church because we are really friendly and have great church suppers," or "Give a big offering so you can be blessed." Our message is not "Touch your television set so you can be healed" or our "God is a really nice guy!" The message of the hour is "Repent and be baptized for the remission of your sins!"

It is to this end that I offer the last chapter.

6 | Jesus Wants to Kill You

Sometimes the preacher will stand at the altar and say, "Come to the Cross and find life!" This is not true.

The cross doesn't give life—the cross takes life.

There is no life to be found in the cross. Only death is found at the cross.

The cross kills.

The cross executes.

The cross slays whatever is put upon it.

One does not come to the cross to find life, but to die.

When we truly give ourselves over to the Lordship of Jesus Christ, we are asking Him to kill everything in us that prevents us from standing before the Father. At the moment we kneel before His cross, the Spirit of God begins to kill within us everything that is of Adam.

He wants to kill our old desires.
He wants to kill our old values
He is putting to death our bitterness, our rebellion,

our grudges, our anger, our lust.
He is destroying the residue of the world within us.

Jesus commands us to take up our cross. Let it put us to death every day to put to the death the old nature, the nature of our father Adam who in his own sin condemned us all.

The cross is laid on every Christian. The first Christ-suffering which every man must experience is the call to abandon the attachments of this world. It is that dying of the old man which is the result of his encounter with Christ. As we embark upon discipleship, we surrender ourselves to Christ in union with his death—we give over our lives to death. Thus, it begins; the cross is not the terrible end to an otherwise god-fearing and happy life, but it meets at the beginning of our communion with Christ. When Christ calls a man, he bids him come and die. It may be a death like that of the first disciples who had to leave home and work to follow him, or it may be a death like Luther's, who had to leave the monastery to go out into the world. But it is the same death every time, death in Jesus Christ, the death of the old man at his call" (Translated from the German NACHFOLGE first published 1937 by Chr. Kaiser Verlag Miinchcn by R. H. Fuller, with some revision by Irmgard Booth. (First edition published 1949 Dietrich Bonhoeffer, The Cost of Discipleship, p 99).

The cross of which Jesus spoke was not a metaphor. It was not a mold for a piece of jewelry.

It was not a decoration on the wall behind a pulpit, nor was it a lofty icon to rest high upon the steeple. The cross of which Jesus spoke had only one purpose: It was an instrument of death, and to take up one's cross is to identify with His death.

I understand that it's a shocking title: *Jesus Wants to Kill You*. It goes against any image or idea we have ever formed of Christ. What a ludicrous, offensive, and completely ridiculous suggestion to make. Jesus is the life-giver, the joy-giver, the breath-giver, the water of life, the bread of life. He is the deliverer, the chain-breaker, sent by the Father that all who believe might live. It is a ridiculous suggestion, except...it is true. Jesus wants to kill you. I have chosen to finish this book with such an outrageous suggestion so that we can comprehend the severity of our sin and the severity with which God deals with sin. So, hang on.

Saul of Tarsus. He was a Pharisee of Pharisees, born of the Tribe of Benjamin, schooled under the hand of the master, Gamaliel. Saul had stood by as a young man, holding the coats of the elders as they stoned the deacon, Stephen. With a zeal unmatched in the land, Saul had pursued the followers of Jesus to every corner of the land. With arrest warrants in his pouch and hatred in heart, Saul drove his horse toward Damascus. These Christians were traitors to the faith. He would see them imprisoned or hung. This cult would not survive.

Without warning everything changed. A deafening clap of thunder and a flash of lightning out of a clear desert sky caused Saul's horse to rear in terror, tossing the man to the ground. Blinded by the bright light, Saul tried to rise from the ground as a shimmering figure emerged from the midst of the light calling his name, "Saul, Saul, why are you persecuting me?" On that fateful day, while on a murderous mission to Damascus, a man by the name of Saul fell to the earth. He was confronted by a dead man, and in that moment Saul himself died.

Out of the dust of that desert road a new man arose, changed by an encounter with the Living Christ. The enemy of the newly birthed church would become its champion. The man who wanted to kill Christians for their faith was dead. Paul, the apostle would himself die by the executioner's sword—changed in a moment.

In a letter to the Christians at Philippi, Paul declares that he has turned his back on everything, all of his accomplishments, his status, reputation, education—everything, in order to obtain a single goal. He declares that goal:

"That I may know him, and the power of his resurrection, and the fellowship of his sufferings, being made conformable unto his death; if by any

means I might attain unto the resurrection of the dead." (Philippians 3:10 ESV)

All that had been important to Saul died in the dust of the Damascus Road. This is repentance, and this is the only way a man may find life in Christ.

"For whoever would save his life will lose it, but whoever loses his life for my sake will find it." (Matthew 16:25 ESV)

A lot of us can get excited about the prospect of the resurrection. We all want to pass through those huge gates of pearl in the New Jerusalem where we will walk on streets of gold and enjoy the grandeur and majesty of a new heaven and a new earth. We long to see loved ones who have died. Won't it be amazing to keep company with the likes of Abraham, Moses, David, and Peter, Paul, and James. The prospect of going to Heaven and spending eternity with Jesus is so exciting! However, we often fail to realize that the pathway to the resurrection leads directly through the cross. Those who will attain to the resurrection must first die for there can be no resurrection without a death.

Much later, Paul would write these words:

"But whatever gain I had, I counted as loss for the sake of Christ. Indeed, I count everything as loss because of the surpassing worth of knowing Christ Jesus my Lord. For his sake I have suffered

the loss of all things and count them as rubbish, in order that I may gain Christ and be found in him, not having a righteousness of my own that comes from the law, but that which comes through faith in Christ, the righteousness from God that depends on faith— that I may know him and the power of his resurrection, and may share his sufferings, becoming like him in his death, that by any means possible I may attain the resurrection from the dead." (Philippians 3:7-14 ESV)

You may be hoping for the resurrection, but Adam is still alive in you. You want eternal life in heaven, but you still cling to the life of the flesh here. Come to the cross and die. Let it kill that which is of Adam in you so that the promise of Scripture will be yours: "Therefore, if anyone is in Christ, he is a new creation. The old has passed away; behold, the new has come." (2 Corinthians 5:17 ESV)

Men clamor and fawn today over a gospel that promises a resurrection without the discomfort of death. This gospel promises us forgiveness without repentance, cleansing without confession, reformation without transformation, and eternal life without a cross. This gospel says you can go to heaven and live forever, bearing in you the old, adamic, sinful nature. You look better, but on the inside that old man still lives. If you plan to stand before a holy God in such a condition, you will die.

George sat on the edge of his bed. In one hand he held a quart of whiskey. In the other, a revolver. He had been arrested yet again for public drunkenness and he was to ashamed to face anyone. In the other room was George's wife and their disabled son, George Jr.

Jr. was their third child and the only one that had survived. He was born with severe disabilities and expected to live only a few weeks. Jr. was now 24 years old. George and Sandy had faithfully cared for their son. George had also spent Jr's entire life drunk. He was mad. He was mad at himself, mad at life, and mad at God. He had always dreamed of having a son with whom he could hunt and fish and do all the things that fathers do with their sons. George felt cheated. George felt great pain. To cover the pain, he drank.

George sat on the edge of the bed drinking, hoping to get drunk enough to have the courage to put the gun in his mouth and pull the trigger. He was embarrassed. He was ashamed of himself and he was sick of his miserable life.

After a while, George sat the bottle down and raised the gun up to his mouth. With tears in his eyes he slowly put pressure on the trigger when suddenly from the other room, Jr. shouted at the top of his lungs, "Daddy!" George Jr. in his 24 years of life had never spoken an intelligible word, but in that instant when his father was poised on the brink of suicide, something rose up in that poor disfigured body. It was like a clap of thunder on the Damascus Road, shocking George sober.

He put down the gun, screwed the cap on the bottle of whiskey and stumbled into the living room of their house trailer. He fell on his knees and put his face in his wife's lap and through hot tears exclaimed, "I need help!" George Jr. never spoke another word after that night, and his father never again put a bottle to his lips. George says, *"God knew what I needed to hear, when I needed to hear it, and who I needed to hear it from."*

Within a week, George was in a rehab center and to this day, he has remained sober. He is an elder in his church and has helped countless men on the road to wholeness through Christ. He leads a vibrant ministry to nearby nursing facilities and has traveled all over the world preaching the gospel of Christ.

George the drunkard died that night and rising out of the ashes of a broken life was a new man, transformed by the power of the gospel. This is repentance. It is not reformation, it is transformation. It is not turning over a new leaf, it is dying to the old self, crucifying the old life, turning away from my life that I might find life in Christ.

"I have been crucified with Christ. It is no longer I who live, but Christ who lives in me. And the life I now live in the flesh I live by faith in the Son of God, who loved me and gave himself for me." (Galatians 2:20 ESV)

Drunkard, Jesus doesn't want to sober you up—He wants to kill you.

Addict, Jesus doesn't want to clean you up—He wants to kill you.

He doesn't want to reassign your gender or turn your sexual orientation—He wants to kill you.

Brawler, fornicator, adulterer, hypocrite, murderer, or harlot; it is not Jesus' plan to reform you — He plans to kill you!

The self-righteous, bitter, angry, lustful, greedy—He wants to kill you, too.

Then, through the power of His resurrection He wants to raise you up to a new life. He wants to cleanse you by the power of His blood. He wants to transform you through the power of His Spirit so that you will no longer be dead in your sins, no longer will you be a wretched, dying son of Adam. You are now a son of God who can approach the Throne of God with boldness because that which was of the first Adam in you is dead, killed by the power of the cross. Now you are alive in the Last Adam.

On the day of Pentecost, the men of Jerusalem cried out to Peter and the others, *"Brothers, what shall we do?"* (Acts 2:37 ESV)

Peter's answer was sharp like a knife, *"Repent and be baptized, every one of you, in the name of Jesus Christ for the forgiveness of your sins. And you will receive the gift of the Holy Spirit. The promise is for you and your children and for all who are far off— for all whom the Lord our God will call."* (Acts 2:38-39 ESV)

This promise, made so long ago, is for you as well.

What will you do?

ABOUT THE AUTHOR

M.K. GANTT

Michael Gantt has been preaching the gospel for more than 50 years. He is a zealous defender of the authority and integrity of the Word of God and a staunch defender of the Biblically defined family.

He served as Senior Pastor of the Agape Christian Fellowship in Brattleboro, Vermont for almost 38 years before stepping aside for his eldest son, Michael Bryan, to step into the role of Lead Pastor.

Pastor Gantt remains active in the church as well as traveling widely speaking in various venues from local churches to national Christian Writers Conferences in Colorado and Philadelphia.

Michael writes under the name of M.K. Gantt and is the author of four other books including:

EDDIE – *Adventures with a 41-Year-Old Motor Home and the Lessons We Learned from Him.*

MAKUTANO – *Lives Intersecting to Write God's Story,* and anthology of stories from three decades of ministry in Africa.

CRY MERCY – *America's Only Hope May Be in Her Destruction.*

SLEEPING NEAR THE ARK - *Writing with a Fresh Vision.* Co-authored with Barbara E. Haley. Lessons from the Prophet Samuel. Written especially for aspiring writers, but powerful principles for anyone involved in Christian ministry.

All books can be ordered from Amazon.com and on Michael's Gantt's website at www.mkgantt.com/books.

Contact Michael Gantt to engage for ministry:

Michael Gantt

539 Western Avenue

Brattleboro, VT 05301

(802)579-6681

mkg@mkgantt.com

Made in the USA
Middletown, DE
23 April 2019